C.A.R.E.S.

THE KEY TO A SUCCESSFUL SUNDAY CHURCH SCHOOL

ROBERT G. and
DEBRA FULGHUM BRUCE

Lima, Ohio
C.S.S. Publishing Company

C.A.R.E.S. — THE KEY TO A SUCCESSFUL SUNDAY CHURCH SCHOOL

Library of Congress Catalog Card Number: 83-073127

Library of Congress Cataloging in Publication Data

Bruce, Robert G., 1949-
C.A.R.E.S.: the key to successful Sunday church school.

1. Sunday-school teachers. 2. Christian education.
I. Bruce, Debra Fulghum, 1951- . II. Title.
III. Title: CARES.
BV1534.B74 1984 268 83-73127
ISBN 0-89536-672-X (pbk.)

1984/ISBN 0-89536-672-X PRINTED IN U.S.A.

Table of Contents

Introduction

This book is for you — whether you are a teacher, pastor, superintendent, or interested lay person in the church; whether you are trained in the field of Christian education, have a background in teaching, or are thinking about becoming involved in your Sunday church school program; whether your beliefs are "conservative," "liberal," or "neither of the above" — this book is for *you!*

This book is about success! Success is defined as a favorable result, a good fortune. And, truly, success is being seen in local churches today. Success stories can vary. Success can mean new prospects for your Sunday church school classes, a deeper commitment from the present members, or activation of those who have fallen away. Success could mean a greater response in your Sunday church school program with more class service projects, care for shut-ins, or on-going visitation teams. And success could involve training more laypersons as leaders in your church's educational program, thus expanding the potential of your present classes and groups.

One 2,000 member church in Jacksonville, Florida, realized success in the Sunday church school program as they increased their attendance by two hundred people on Sunday morning. A three hundred member church in a rural town experienced success when the only adult class embarked on a mission of faith and sponsored a Haitian family for one year. And a church in Iowa met with success with the purchase of a van that carries persons from Handicap Village to Sunday church school each week.

Using the formula described in this book, churches are finding success in Christ's church — both qualitatively and quantitatively. Yet, no matter how the term is defined, one fact remains — *success* can happen in your Sunday church school!

This book is also about personal caring. The essence of the New Testament lies in the fact that God loved us so much that he gave us his only son, Jesus. Jesus Christ lived a life of love and caring for mankind. Because God loved us, we are free to love others. Caring is that one ingredient that turns us into special agents for Christ. Not only are we objects of God's love, but when we care for others, we mirror his ever-present grace.

Caring is vital in Christian ministry. As you study the scriptures, pray diligently, and share God's Word with others, you can best fulfill your duty as a teacher if genuine concern toward others is felt. In other words, caring gives meaning to all of the methods and techniques we use as teachers and is vital in developing one's faith. In fact, most people active in the Sunday church school remember that it was a caring teacher who touched their life personally — more than any planned lesson, program, or method.

This book offers a powerful formula for giving teachers and leaders in the local church new insight into a balanced, successful educational ministry. Psychologists claim that certain traits are common among human beings. Maslow's theory points to several needs that are basic to human personality. Among those are:

1. *the need to be loved,*
2. *the need to belong,*
3. *the need for self-worth.*

Using the formula in this book, teachers in the local church can fulfill these basic needs and others through personal caring, including:

1. *loving each individual,*
2. *helping class members feel ownership of the class,*
3. *finding potential in each person.*

This book outlines a proven, step-by-step program for involving this personal caring in a balanced educational ministry, a Christ-centered ministry filled with his agape love. Each chapter is complete with practical, how-to methods which you can use in your class or Sunday church school program. And these methods are geared toward success; they have brought proven results to other Christian educators and teachers.

Most people attend Sunday church school for fellowship. Not only do members receive nurture and training, but Sunday church school classes provide small groups where caring and friendships are found. New Testament Christians called this *koinonia* — the community where love and acceptance are experienced. On the same note, most people quit Sunday church school classes because of lack of caring and fellowship. "No one ever knew my name," one woman in my church shared. Another man said, "I never felt needed in my class, so why go?"

The Bible challenges us to know each other's names, to care for one another. In John 10:3b, we find, "And the sheep hear his voice: and he calleth his own sheep by name, and leadeth them out." We can mentally picture the worn shepherd keeping track of all the furry sheep, large and small, young and old, as they enter the pasture for grazing. Most shepherds verify that if *one* sheep becomes lost or hurt along the way, he will leave the flock to go comfort it.

As a teacher and leader in Christ's church, you are called upon to be a shepherd. You are the gatekeeper who is responsible for the members of your sheepfold, the members in your class. Not only are you commissioned to teach the Word of God, you are also instructed to heal the wounds, celebrate the victories, and provide opportunities for response with your students. Matthew 12:12 reminds us, "How much then is a man better than a sheep." The importance of caring among God's people is clear.

Finally, this book is about results! Using the formula C.A.R.E.S., you can experience proven success in your Sunday church school program. While the Bible is primarily a love story of God's self-giving love revealed in his son Jesus Christ, it is also a success story. The Bible proclaims man's victory through God in conquering oppression, despair, turmoil, and most importantly, death. In 2 Corinthians 2:14, we read "Thanks be to God, which causeth us to triumph in Christ." Triumph. Success. These two celebration words go hand-in-hand. But before you can experience this triumph, you must

1. *Begin where you are with a personal and class inventory,*
2. *Read the basic formula for Sunday church school success in chapters one through five,*
3. *Set long- and short-term goals for your class success,*
4. *Use the creative program helps to further your education program.*

The, as you *care*fully and *prayer*fully attempt to strengthen your educational program, the triumph will be yours as lives are touched by the love of our Lord.

Personal Inventory

The following inventory is designed to help you gain insight into your past experiences with the local church, as well as to identify your present strengths and weaknesses as a church member and leader.

Reflect on the past

1. Did you ever have a negative attitude toward Sunday church school as a child? Why?
2. Did you have a positive attitude toward a Sunday church school class? Can you describe this?

3. Can you recall a certain teacher or leader who touched your life? Exactly how did this happen?
4. Did a Sunday church school teacher ever visit in your home? phone you? send you a card or letter?
5. Did you ever confide a sorrow or joy to your teacher?
6. Was a classroom teacher ever consistently late? unprepared?
7. Was a specific teacher ever creative or innovative in teaching methods?
8. Can you recall a teacher who shared a personal faith with you?

Identify with the present

1. Do you completely understand your job description as a teacher, leader, or director in the Sunday church school?
2. Do you enjoy what you are doing?
3. Why did you accept this position?
4. Do you use a specific curriculum with which to teach?
5. Do you know every student's name?
6. How many times have you had a class party or social this year?
7. Do you understand the age-level characteristics of your age group? the needs?
8. Do you try to use extra resources, films, and speakers to complement the lesson?
9. Do you spend at least an hour a week preparing the lesson?
10. Do you see yourself as a meaningful leader in the eyes of those you teach?
11. Do you have a positive, accepting attitude toward your calling as a teacher, leader, or director?

Rate Yourself

LOW		***AVERAGE***		***HIGH***
1	**2**	**3**	**4**	**5**

1. My understanding of the Bible.

2. My personal prayer life.
3. My confidence in sharing my faith with others.
4. My ability to communicate and teach the written word.
5. My understanding of my denomination's curriculum.
6. My ability to relate personally to class members.
7. My participation in other activities in our church.
8. My enthusiasm for teaching.
9. My enthusiasm for my faith.

Class Inventory

1. What percentage of your total class membership attends each week?
2. What is the group's response to your teaching methods?
3. Is there active discussion and participation each week?
4. How is the class's enthusiasm?
5. How many inactive members are there on your roll?
6. Have decisions been made for Christ in your class?
7. Is there an on-going service project?
8. Do your students participate in homework or study the lesson each week?
9. Are the members of the class actively caring for one another?
10. Are the members involved in the life of the total church?
11. Is the pastor a supportive person in the Sunday church school program?

[You may wish to photocopy the inventories and share this discovery with other teachers or class members.]

How Did You Score?

What was the result of your inventory? Did you rate high on concern, but low on social involvement? Are you lacking in an understanding of God's Word, yet full of enthusiasm for the Christian faith? Does your class need some motivation to become more involved in the activities of your local church? Whatever the case, the next five chapters have answers for you!

Chapter One

CONCERN
The Role of The Caring Teacher

"Did you notice in the newspaper today that a Janet Nelson died?" Rob Davis asked his wife, Lynette. "Do you think she is the same Janet Nelson that is related to the child in our Sunday church school class?"

"Oh, I doubt it," Lynette replied. "But we can certainly find out."

She then proceeded to call the pastor and discovered it was true — this woman was the mother of Chuck Nelson, a fifth grade student in their class. She had died after a lengthy illness at a young age of thirty-five.

"I feel terrible," Lynette cried as she placed the receiver down. "Here I have been riding hard on Chuck these past few weeks for misbehaving in the classroom, when he was actually expressing his insecurity. I wish I had taken time to find out why he was acting that way."

"Same here," Rob agreed. "But what we need to do now is go to the home. Perhaps we can show our concern by helping with the children."

Later that day the Davises went to the Nelson home and visited with Chuck. Lynette offered to help with preparing food for the family while Rob played games with the younger children, so that Mr. Nelson could make arrangements. Even though they had been unaware of past crises in the family, their immediate concern was helpful in comforting the grieving family.

People showing concern. Sometimes this is a difficult task; sincere concern takes time, energy, and, in some cases, is emotionally draining. Still, concern is the basis for a caring Christian ministry.

Many years ago a few persons were concerned enough about children to start what we now know as "Sunday church school." Sunday church school beginnings stem back to 1780 with a Gloucester, England, newspaperman named Robert Raikes. Raikes was so concerned about local children being deprived of an education that he hired teachers to give educational and moral training on Sunday mornings.

There are people like Raikes who are still concerned about Christian education. And it is this same concern that is touching lives for Christ in the local church. Why? Because concern is necessary for a teacher and student to develop a close relationship through which the love of God can be shared.

Christ believed in the principle that a small group of well-trained disciples could permeate a larger group in much the same way that a little yeast in the dough leavens the whole loaf. (Luke 13:21) Jesus not only taught this principle, he also put it into practice in the training of the twelve. It was through the investment of himself in an intimate, instructive, purposeful relationship that Jesus equipped the twelve. Through the course of a few years, he trained them by indelibly stamping their lives with a model of ministry they could not forget.[1]

As teachers we must also indelibly stamp lives within our classroom. Our concern for others must be so intimate, so full of selfless love, that people know we are authentic. "Ye yourselves are taught of God to love one another." (1 Thessalonians 4:9) Still, the questions remain: When do I show concern? How do I let others know I am sincerely concerned for them? How do I find out who is hurting?

Years ago, while serving on the staff of a large church, I was involved in leading the youth program. As I was handed my job description, I was also given a lengthy roster of inactive members.

"Why, there are over one hundred names on this inactive list," I said in disbelief. I looked at the others at the education meeting and asked, "Where are all of these young people?"

"Well," the superintendent said, "many came for just a few weeks with a friend. Then we never heard from them again. Some have just drifted away, yet their parents have remained active."

The answers bothered me "Never came back" . . . "Drifted away." Somewhere, some young people were feeling alone, afraid, empty, and no one even knew who they were. Realizing the need to care for God's people, I made up my mind at that moment that my ministry would be "to find the lost sheep."

The first young man I contacted was obviously unenthusiastic about my phone call.

"Is this Steven?" I tried to sound cheerful.

"Yeah," was the dull response.

"Well, this is your Sunday church school teacher," I was positive as I made my introduction.

"Sunday church school teacher?" The response was even more startled. "Oh, yeah."

"I just wanted you to know that we are beginning a new study next Sunday and I would like to see you come," I continued, not letting his apathy get me down.

"O.K. I might," was his nonchalant reply.

I hung up the phone feeling so dejected and alone. "I might?" Is this the type of commitment I am going to receive? But, then, realizing my tremendous task, I continued dialing numbers in my search for the lost members.

After four weeks of aggressive concern — phone calls, home visits, cards in the mail — the youth class had tripled its attendance. But still no Steven.

I tried again each week calling this young man. And each week his voice sounded more apathetic and distant. I went to go see him, yet, his school activities and part-time job kept him unavailable.

I had almost given up on Steven, when one Sunday morning as I was waiting for the members of my class to arrive, a tall, dark-haired young man walked into the classroom and plopped himself in an overstuffed chair opposite me.

"Good morning." I looked up in surprise. "I am your teacher. And, you are . . ."

"I know who you are," the youth said with a large grin. "I am Steven. I came so you would quit bugging me with your phone calls."

We both laughed aloud as I admitted that perhaps I had been "buggy." But what had actually happened is that this persistent concern had touched one life. The young man was present every Sunday from that day on, and even joined the evening fellowship group and youth choir. Why? Simply because someone cared enough not to give up on him; someone took time to find the lost sheep.

The shepherd leaves the flock when one goes astray. His love is stamped on each sheep and his endless concern proves this as "he calleth his own sheep by name." (John 10:3b) A teacher must also show concern for each class member and this means more than just knowing the student's name and address.

How To Show Real Concern

Step One: Know Your Students

Concern begins with building relationships. And in the Sunday church school classroom, relationships are usually formed after church hours. This could be in visiting the home, meeting the person for a cola or a cup of coffee, or calling on the phone. Meeting with your class members on their territory enables you to see where they are in their walk with the Lord; determine if they are having problems in their home life; and learn of their personal interests, hobbies, likes, and dislikes.

Bill Andrews, a teacher of the adult class in a large southern church, prefers to invite different class members over to his home for Sunday dinner.

"We reserve Sunday for entertaining the members of the class," Bill shared with a group of teachers in his conference. "I invite a few members the week before so they can plan on this, and rotate the list so everyone gets a turn. The rewards are terrific! Because people get to know me personally, they take a true interest in the class. I guess the Bible becomes real as they see my caring for them."

Another young minister who directs a youth program in Margate, Florida, tells of his success in meeting with young people on their turf:

"I have permission to take the church van to the main high school on Wednesdays during the school lunch break," he said enthusiastically. "The members of my youth group gather their friends and pile into the van for a Brown Bag Study. We picnic in a nearby park; then I lead a sharing group and Bible study. The response is tremendous. I am living my concern for them, and their commitment to Christ and the church is resulting."

Quality time spent with each person — child, youth, adult — in your classroom is especially important in order for you to meet their personal needs in the class lessons. *Persistence* is also important, so that you don't give up in caring for the "lost sheep." And this concern must be on-going. In other words, you cannot make one call per member each quarter and expect that to be sufficient. Only as you show concern over and over again, does believability occur. The student will begin to perceive your approach as genuine and you will be accepted as a true friend.

To care for another person, you must be able to understand him and his world as if you were inside it. You must be able to see, as it were, with his eyes what his world is like to him and how he sees it himself.[2] "Be ye all of one mind, having compassion one of another, love as brethren." (1 Peter 3:8) Teachers must exhibit this self-less, agape love as they strive to understand the class members.

Effective Tools

Tool #1 — Record Keeping

In order effectively to show concern for each class member, the teacher must be efficient and organized in keeping records. A 3x5 file box with cards for names of class members, inactives, and visitors is useful for this. On the file cards, write pertinent information such as name, address, phone number, birthdates, and any other personal knowledge. Leave space on the back of each card for comments you may have pertaining to the person. For example, if you call or visit Ray Smith and he appears uninterested in the class, write down this insight. But also follow through in keeping lines of communication open with Ray by visiting or phoning him regularly. As his attitude changes or new insights are seen, list this on the personal space.

Tool #2 — Class Directory

Another helpful aid in becoming a concerned teacher is a class directory. This can be formed using snapshots and a brief summary of each person in the class. A class directory may tell important dates, names of family members, educational and religious backgrounds, and personal interests. Not only does this directory aid the teacher in becoming aware of specific needs, it also helps the other class members to be informed and knowledgeable about one another.

Tool #3 — Class Bulletin Board

A teacher can help spread concern for each member by using a bulletin board in the classroom. On this board you may list prayer needs, honor someone with a current birthday or anniversary, or tell of a class member's specific achievement.

Tool #4 — Personal Letters

There is nothing more touching than a handwritten letter on personal stationery. Sending several letters each week to various members helps you to convey a message of concern. Perhaps the letter is to a member undergoing family problems, someone who contributed to the discussion on Sunday morning, or simply to say "have a nice day." The result will be a class member who feels special and loved.

Tool #5 — Caring Persons

When a class has over eight members, it is best to assign several "caring persons" to help the teacher in keeping in touch with the membership. Assign five or six names to each "caring person." This person has the responsibility to call people in his group of names, those who for some reason are not in class, and relay any pertinent information to the teacher and pastor. No one can get lost in a large Sunday church school class if "caring persons" are responsible for others.

Other effective tools you can use to show concern include:

- Sending cards to inactive persons, birthday honorees, or just "happy day" cards.
- Ongoing visitation each week by the teacher and several class members.
- Telephoning absent members each week.
- Providing transportation to Sunday church school or other church activities for those who are unable to drive — children, youth, and adults.
- Praying for each class member daily and selecting prayer partners for the group.

Step Two: Know Yourself

In showing concern for others, it is important that you do not lose yourself. Although a class member may have tremendous trials to contend with, your job is to care for and to listen to — not to worry and lose faith. For a classroom teacher, it is important that you realize this as you strive for authenticity. Do not try to be something you are not while trying to be a real person.

One such teacher — I'll call him Frank — experienced this as he became overwhelmed with a student's problems.

"I got so absorbed in a young man's family problems that I let my own spiritual life suffer," Frank confessed. "I guess I felt that I had all the answers. I would leave work to go counsel with the boy, spend my dinner time with his family trying to smooth the conflict, and stay awake all night trying to find solutions. It finally got to me. My family was suffering, my job was overbearing, and I had to leave the church for awhile to rediscover my priorities."

Concern is the key to being a successful teacher, and healthy concern does not mean becoming so overwhelmed by a member's problems that you ignore yourself and loved ones. You need to know your weaknesses, strengths, abilities, and disabilities, lest you wind up like Frank.

In caring for others, in helping them grow, you actualize yourself. The writer grows in caring for his ideas; the teacher grows in caring for his students; the parent grows in caring for his child. Or, put differently, by using resources such as trust, understanding, courage, responsibility, devotion, and honesty, you grow also; and you are able to bring such resources into play because your interest is focused on the other.[3]

Others learn about concern by watching you. The ways you show concern for class members give that important pattern they will slowly pick up and establish in their own lives. How you contend with a family problem, community relationships, and other matters in your church reinforces priorities that you have spoken of as being true.

A young college girl shared that she had attended a friend's church while visiting her friend's home during the holidays.

"Connie had told me what a marvelous teacher she had for Sunday church school, 'really caring' is how she described him," the young girl spoke. "But when I got to the class, I noticed a retarded student walking through the door into the class. Can you believe this 'caring' teacher made a face of disgust behind that student's back? I didn't hear a word of the lesson because I felt he was a phony."

A young father expressed his feeling for a Sunday church school teacher he had as a child. "Mrs. Pearcy represented God to me. I looked up to her. Her voice was kind, but firm. Her hands were smooth, but strong. And her faith and love were lasting, no matter what went on in the classroom."

As a teacher in the Sunday church school, you are often the best Christian your students know. To some, you even represent God. It sounds like a heavy burden to carry. But if you take time to truly get to know yourself, then you can accept your inner being and move into the world as being really "you."

How do you get to know yourself? In Matthew 5:3-10, Christ gives us eight keys to the Kingdom of God, a kingdom that can be experienced now.

1. Blessed are the poor in spirit.

To be poor in spirit means that you can risk admitting that you do not have all the answers. Then you can freely affirm God as the strength and wisdom in your life.

Stan, the men's Bible teacher in a small church, shared this story: "I used to hesitate in expressing my personal feelings with my class. But I have realized that I can honestly say 'I don't know' without endangering my teaching credentials. In fact, my students feel closer to me and to God as I suggest that we turn to him for answers."

2. Blessed are those who mourn.

Do you show empathy to your class members when they express a doubt or concern? Do you try to feel what they are feeling? If someone is experiencing trials, listen to their problems. Let them know you also experience loneliness and pain as they do. Then offer the hope of our Christian faith to fill these times of pain and sorrow.

3. Blessed are the meek.

Are you a "take charge" teacher, or do you let others have ownership in the classroom? Often, in the midst of our enthusiasm to do God's work, we need to sit back and give credit to him for the successes. The saying "let go and let God" is most meaningful in striving for meekness.

4. Blessed are those who hunger and thirst for righteousness.

Open your mind to the miracles of God. Do you let God communicate to you through daily prayer, Bible study, and meditation? If so, you will be filled with insight into living. Only by filling yourself will you be able to give to others.

5. *Blessed are the merciful.*

To have mercy or concern is the key to success in the local church. Once you can acquire the caring habit, you will experience the rewards of seeing lives change with his love. If you show genuine mercy, the response will be commitment to Christ.

6. *Blessed are the pure in heart.*

To be able to see the "good" in life is the ability of the pure in heart. This means finding God in the midst of trial and heartache. It also means finding the good or potential in each individual in the classroom. If you can model being genuine and pure in heart, your class will receive the benefit of seeing Christian freedom in action.

7. *Blessed are the peacemakers.*

Jesus intended for us to make peace — not just keep peace in the world. This often involves speaking the truth in love and compromising if there is conflict. The Christian faith is one of the choices. You are responsible for standing up for these right choices as you face rebuttal from challengers.

8. *Blessed are those who are persecuted for righteousness sake.*

No one ever said that the Christian life would be easy. Often you will be called upon to make decisions using knowledge you have gained from the Bible. And often this will not be a popular position. You may even encounter repercussions from class members. If so, you will not be the first Christian to have experienced this. Keep in mind the eternal rewards as you contend with conflict from non-believers and keep absorbed in studying the Word as you gather strength from your Heavenly Father.

Getting to know yourself involves opening yourself up to God's will as you prepare the lesson each week. Prayer, quiet time, study time, and meditation all help to find answers as to how God can use you in his service. Once you feel comfortable in accepting yourself, you can begin to take risks, expose your personal feelings during class time, and share your faith in God.

Step Three: Know God

Jesus said, "Feed my sheep." (John 21:16) Although most animals are able to hunt out feeding grounds, those who know sheep tell us they are helpless and must be led to their food. As the Sunday church school teacher, you are responsible for leading your class to the feeding grounds found in God's Word. But you must first nurture your own personal relationship with God before you can show the way. As you live the Bible day by day, you are able to offer insight and application as "food for thought" in the classroom. How ironic it is when the teacher neglects this every day relationship with the Father: the class can only suffer as emptiness and apathy are conveyed. In fact, teachers will only be able to meet the concerns of students as they saturate themselves with God and God's Word. *You must first become a learner before you can be a teacher.*

D. K. Reisinger says, "Much Bible study without prayer may lead to pride. Prayer without Bible study may lead to fanaticism. But proper balance between Bible study and prayer will produce a well-rounded Christian with a valid, effective testimony."[4]

Tool # 1 — Daily Bible Study

Your number one duty as a teacher is your personal relationship with God. Nothing should interfere with this, for before you can tell of God's Word, you must know God's Word.

Set aside a specific time each day to study your Bible. This is apart from your curriculum study. Bible study is reading to *fill* your life. Keep pencil and paper handy, and jot down new discoveries, questions, and scriptures that would be beneficial to your life.

Tool #2 — Ongoing Prayer

Prayer is communication with God. If you don't talk with

someone, you can't get to know them. Therefore, you must talk to God daily. Tell God your problems, praise him for his mighty works on earth, thank him for his gifts to you, and pray for others constantly.

As you pray, be sure to listen. God may be revealing answers to you when you least expect them. And, follow through on these "spiritual hunches" you may experience.

Tool #3 — Daily Meditation

Meditation requires being alone. It could include a walk around the block for fresh air, listening to quiet music on the stereo, or cloud-gazing in the backyard. Being alone gives you time to sort through your life goals, make important decisions, and allow God to work through your mind.

Tool #4 — Daily Journal Entries

A journal is a compilation of your personal thoughts, experiences, worries, dreams, and joys. As you make time for study each day, take five minutes and write entries in your journal. You may describe insecure feelings you had that day. You may write an anecdote or story that occurred at church. Or, you may write about a theological problem that you are dealing with.

A journal can help you to communicate with yourself, thus get to know yourself even better. As you keep these daily notes, you can read back through from time to time and measure your Christian growth. You may wish to share this personal growth with class members as you see your life hurdles conquered.

Tool #5 — Listening to Others

Often God moves through others. Keep closely attuned to friends, family members, and other Christians for new insights into the faith. And keep an open mind as growth may occur for you.

A teacher who reaches the goal of knowing the students, knowing self, and knowing God is on the road to Christian success in this calling. But there is still more to being concerned than merely reaching out. A concerned teacher must also:

1. *Be a team member — a co-worker with Christ.* Teaching is not a contest. Rather, it is a team of chosen disciples working together for the glory of God. Remember this as you share your insights, resources, joys, and concerns with other church leaders.

2. *Be above pettiness and gossip.* During World War II it was said that "loose lips sink ships." Teachers must be above negativism as they influence many lives. If you have a complaint with your church, air it positively with someone in authority and keep communication open. Don't criticize and tear down God's Kingdom with verbal abuse.

3. *Arrive early and be prepared to greet the students personally.* A student should never — *never!* — arrive before the teacher. A dark, cold classroom looks dark and cold. Make a point to get there before the early birds in order to convey an environment of love.

4. *Be tactful and diplomatic in handling problems.* If conflict arises during class time, encourage compromise and openness. You must be the overseer in the class, making sure that no one is being stepped on or discriminated against. In other words, you must have eyes in front and back of your head.

5. *Be enthusiastic!* If you are "filled with God" and radiate his love, others will capture this spirit.

6. *Pray each week.* Prayer is vital in the classroom as we ask for God's guidance in our teaching.

7. *Tell of moments when God became real to you.* Your class will feel honored that you care enough to share your spiritual secrets. They will respond with openness.

8. *Use a variety of teaching methods.* Try not to become bogged down with one particular method. As you creatively apply Bible passages to new teaching methods, your students will respond with enthusiasm.

9. *Encourage ownership in the class.* This could be done by finding a small task in the class for each class member. Ownership is vital in order for members to continue the commitment they made to the class.

Through the Sunday church school class. concerned persons are able to serve God by caring for one another. In the Dart Class at a large church, a group of active church members have grown up together. It was these same people who met in homes over thirty years ago when the charter for the church was written. Through the years, the members have seen babies and grandbabies born, have attended family weddings and funerals, and have shared in one another's joys and sorrows. On Sunday morning a typical greeting might be "Did you hear if Martha was getting out of the hospital yet?" Or, "Did Bob get to go see his grandchildren at Christmas?" This class is not just a source of curriculum information, but a resource of love, care, and strength as members truly "know one another." Yet as the class members are asked about this gift of concern, they exclaim, "We learned this love from a teacher we had years ago."

In the magazine *Church School Today*, editor Ruth McDowell describes a vivid memory of her childhood experience. This occurred in Sunday church school in Chelan, Washington, when she was five years old:

"I don't recall the name of the teacher or what she looked like. I do recall a few things that she said, but most of all I remember what she did.

"In the middle of the class session on that particular Sunday the teacher commented that she would have a surprise for us the following Sunday. Shyly I told her that I would not be there because I would be moving with my family to Oklahoma.

" 'Then we will have the surprise today,' she said. And so we did.

"The teacher brought out a set of blocks, and we all worked

together building a wall. As we worked — or perhaps it was before — the teacher talked about a wall in the Bible Times. I am not certain about the characters, but I think the Bible story may have been about Nehemiah and the rebuilding of the Jerusalem wall. Nor do I remember the size of the blocks we used.

"Yes, many of the details are forgotten, but I can still feel the inner glow I experienced when the teacher changed her plans just for *me*. This one small act convinced me that she loved me and that God loved me. I felt very important at that special moment. God loved me, a little child."[5]

Two teachers had radiated concern. This concern was contagious and caught by the many lives in the classroom. The shepherd is the symbol of concern in the Gospels. When we are faced with crises we may quote, "The Lord is my shepherd." This one symbol, of being a shepherd, should be the goal of the Sunday church school teacher.

Each action you display in being a shepherd is met with a reaction from the members of your class. Note the following positive and negative responses.

TEACHER'S ACTION	STUDENT'S RE-ACTION
• Shows concern for individual	• Feels important and becomes interested.
• Shows apathy	• Returns apathy
• Knows students' names, interests, joys, concerns	• Accepts teacher as a disciple of God
• Can't recall many students in the class	• Students drop in attendance
• Sensitive to class needs	• Students develop self-esteem
• Teacher doesn't listen	• Students quit talking

Are you taking action for concern in your classroom? Are the members in your class re-acting positively? People showing concern. That is what successful teaching is all about.

BIBLIOGRAPHY

1. *The Pastor's Church Growth Handbook*, edited by Dr. Win Arn, published by Church Growth Press, Pasaden, California, 1979, page 29.
2. *On Caring*, Milton Mayeroff, Harper and Row Publishers, New York, 1972, pages 41, 42.
3. *On Caring*, page 30.
4. *Leadership*, Spring, 1981, page 10.
5. *Church School*, December 1978, Vol. 11, no. 4, page 1.

Chapter Two

AFFIRMATION

A newborn sleeps in the arms of the nursery teacher. A gregarious preschooler giggles with delight as he hits the rhythm blocks together. A young child works diligently on the creche she will use for a class celebration. A group of teens sing with guitars about their love for God at a morning worship service. Men and women — married, single, widowed, divorced, young, old — study in the adult classes sharing personal joys and concerns with one another.

The church is made up of people. And the life of every person is ultimately in the hands of each of us — to strengthen, to nurture, to affirm. Yet, often we become negligent in our responsibilities as "people builders." "Who has the time to build up class members?" a woman asked honestly at a teacher's retreat. "I work full time, raise two teenagers, and make it to teach my class each Sunday. I don't have time to do anymore."

Some teachers become so involved with *what* to teach, that they forget *who* they are teaching. "I'd rather present the curriculum than get involved with the problems of the class members," Jake said in confidence. "If they ask for help, I will assist. But, to me, people are problems!"

Psychiatrist Karl Menninger says, "The world is made up of people, but people of the world forget this. It is hard to believe that, like ourselves, other people are born of women, reared by parents, teased by brothers . . . consoled by wives . . . flattered by grandchildren, and buried by parsons and priests with the blessings of the church and the tears of those left behind . . . It is easier to speak of fate, and destiny, and waves of the future than to consider the ways we determine our own fate, right now and in the immediate past and future."[1]

People are people and people do have problems as Jake said. Even the Apostle Paul confessed to living in personal conflict when, in Romans 7:18-24, he said, "I know that good does not live in me — that is, in my human nature. For even though the desire to do good is in me, I am not able to do it. I don't do the good I want to do; instead, I do the evil that I do not want to do. If I do what I don't want to do, this means that I am no longer the one who does it; instead, it is the sin that lives in me . . . What an unhappy man I am! Who will rescue me from this body that is taking me to death? Thanks be to God, who does this through our Lord Jesus Christ!"

People living with problems, conflict and inner turmoil: This is the church! Yet, every problem of humankind can be turned into potential if someone cares enough to be an "enabler" to someone else. To "enable" means to bring out, to empower, to help reckon that full potential that is inside each of God's children. It has been said that most of us only realize a fraction of our true potential. Most of what we are all about is hidden deep within us, masked by all of our negative past experiences, our failures, our fears. Yet, as people with problems, we need to be discovered! We need to be seen as more than just something with problems. We need to be heard, to be cared for, to be affirmed, to grow. As the classroom teacher you hold the key to unlocking this hidden potential for your students.

"Persons grow through love. Love has been the theme of religious prophets, ethical teachers, and romantic poets. Now it is becoming the urgent demand of psychologists and social scientists as the weight of evidence accumulates that life without love is fatally crippling. From the unwanted child to the juvenile delinquent to the neurotic adult to the senile decline of the lonely aged person runs a

1. Karl Menninger, (New York: Harcourt Brace & Company, 1942), p. 4.

straight line of loveless despair. Such tragedies are preventable where love is generously available, but where love is wanting, psychological growth is stunted and distorted. "Spare the rod and spoil the child" is a false proverb that has reaped a bitter harvest of neglect, repression, and resentment. A truer view is that to spare the love is to spoil the person of any age. Excesses of love are now better understood as prompted by neurotic fear and possessiveness caused by some earlier denial of love.[2]

Just what is the Sunday church school teacher's role in affirming and believing in each person in the classroom? How deeply does the teacher have to get involved in personal insecurities? Before teachers can start enabling the students in the classroom, they must first look inwardly, to discover their own attitudes, for what you say or how you act or react has a great influence on those around you.

Take the following attitude check-up:

YES	NO	
______	______	When I have to do something I don't want to do, I never complain to others.
______	______	I enjoy trying new methods and let people know of my willingness.
______	______	If someone or something interrupts my plans or train of thought, I accept this and try to re-channel my energies.
______	______	My friends and neighbors know I am a Christian by my enthusiasm for Christ.
______	______	When a family member or friend makes a suggestion about my own behavior or problems, I accept this graciously.
______	______	At the office, at home, at play, at Sunday church

Paul E. Johnson, (Nashville: Abingdon, 1953), p. 30.

school, I have the same attitude toward people.

______ ______ I have an easy time building up those around me.

What did you score? If you chose the "yes" blanks, then your attitude is positive. If you didn't, then read on!

All of us have encountered persons who radiate enthusiasm or a good attitude. An enthusiastic person can enter into a negative situation and motivate positive actions with his leadership and guidance.

When we speak of becoming an enthusiastic teacher helping to affirm or build up those around us, we are talking about becoming inspired by God. In fact, enthusiasm means "filled with God." When you become so inspired your mind, your body, and your soul fills with his love and you begin to share this warmth with others.

The first step in making an attitude change, in becoming enthusiastic and affirming, involves being flexible. Instead of saying No! to new ideas or teaching settings, ask why not? Often we become too comfortable with our traditions and habits and have a difficult time accepting new ideas.

Times are changing in the local church's Sunday church school. People have varying needs and communicate differently than they did thirty years ago. In order to relate effectively with family, friends, and students, you must remain open to innovation in your life.

This does not mean you should always seek for change in your teaching and ministry, but you should keep an open, positive attitude. Be willing to try new ways of communication and new methods of teaching to help spread the Gospel message.

Have an attitude of anticipation in your teaching. Have you ever met someone whose eyes sparkled when they talked? Surely they were exciting to be around as their zest for life was contagious. The song "Something Good is Going to Happen to You" speaks of this type of expectation in daily living. And you can learn to incorporate this attitude in your life as you look for the small, daily miracles. Begin each day with prayer time and ask God for an attitude of wonder. Then, thank God as you experience the small gifts he may give during the day. Learn to see each day and each student in your classroom as something or someone filled with hope and potential. Such an optimistic attitude must come from within.

The final and most important step in changing your attitude into that of an "enabler" is allowing God to use you each day. At work, at play, at home, in the classroom — come prepared to share a living, radiant faith. As you listen with compassion to students and share personal experiences, struggles, and victories, you will be relating how God is changing your life. This openness and concern will help your students to grow from your positive outlook. Be concerned for those people and take time to become personally involved in each students' faith and life struggles.

Jesus said "You are the salt of the earth." (Matthew 5:13a) As a Sunday church school teacher, *you* are the seasoning which can add enthusiasm and a positive attitude to the members of your class.

The teachings of Jesus found in Matthew 25:35-40 offer us insight into how we can truly affirm each individual in Christ's church with whom we are in contact.

1. For I was hungry and you gave me food . . .

Are we open with class members about our own spiritual life? If we pretend to be "Super-Christians" with no problems, we may remain distant to students. "Unapproachable" is a term people use to describe leaders who play a pious, "know-it-all" role. Only by risking being exposed and letting each member know us personally can we encourage growth in others.

Support groups in the education program are an excellent means for affirming people where they are. These groups are formed by small groups of people with common needs, who meet regularly to share ideas and problems, and who find strength within the same group. This unique form of ministry not only provides a means for problems to be answered and faith to be nurtured, it also enables the church members and classroom teachers to reach out to the surrounding community and relate a living Lord to the real concerns of the world.

Different support groups meet different needs. Many groups are concerned with single parents or divorced persons; others are for new mothers or single persons. All over the country active groups help persons with drug, alcohol, or health problems, the terminally ill, and their families, and parents of children of special need.

How does this affirm people and bring out the potential in the individual? "I felt I was the only parent who had a child that was handicapped until I was able to talk about the problems with others in the same situation. When the six parents in my support group shared their personal concerns, fears, and uncertainties, I felt relieved and affirmed. Maybe this won't be so difficult after all!"

Another elderly man shared, "We started a J.O.Y. (Just Older Youth) group in my church for senior citizens. It seems in our youth-oriented society, people look down on the aged. I even felt depressed after retirement until I found a group that made me feel my worth. I enjoy our weekly group outings and sharing times. The leaders in the group believe in the importance of every person — no matter what our age or capabilities."

Can you use support groups in your Sunday church school program to affirm the special needs of class members? Look at some suggestions in organizing such groups.

1. Let the need be known — such as: "All persons who are single parents — widowed, divorced, alone — are invited to a coffee and organizational meeting at the church on Wednesday at 7:00 p.m."

2. Use the media — church newsletters, community bulletin boards, community news on the radio, television, the newspaper, word of mouth, or any other available way to get the message known.

3. Limit the number in the group — usually ten participants in a group is as many as a support group can handle effectively. If you have more interested members, start another group.

4. Involve the pastor — encourage him/her to visit the support groups, making sure an invitation to church is extended to non-members.

5. Select a meeting time, place, room, and date — then, place the information permanently on the church calendar,keeping the lines of communication open with the staff.

6. Select a convener — ask someone familiar with support groups to be present for the first few meetings to help participants get acquainted and get started.

Leaders in the Sunday church school in the local church must remain open to new, innovative ways to affirm the members. Support groups are just one special way of helping people with specific needs. Support groups can also help members find answers for their personal problems. Often, as classroom teachers, we feel we must be the "answer man or woman" for our students. What students do need from us is our genuine openness and concern for them as people of worth. Then, through personal testimony and living a Christ-centered life, we may enable them to build a relationship with our Lord and seek their ultimate potential.

2. I was thirsty and you gave me drink . . .

What is your level of commitment to your task as a classroom teacher? Giving of time and energy is not easy week after week! The teaching job is full of ups and downs as well as sorrow and laughter. Staying with it through the tough times requires commitment.

The challenge of Hebrews 12:1 is this: "Let us run with patience the particular race that God has set before us." This patience involves not giving up the teaching responsibilities when apathy sets in, but "hanging in" and accepting the situation until changes occur.

One teacher in a large church learned this type of patience. "I struggled for one year teaching a large class of fifth grade boys. I did everything by the book — getting to know each child; making sure my class-time was exciting and appealing; preparing my lessons intently each week. But still I felt depressed. I began to feel as though the children were rebelling against me. Finally, after a year, I started to see results. Some of the young guys started to respond to my personal belief in them. They began to show interest and some even changed their obstinate ways into responsible behavior in the classroom."

The Lord's time is not always our time. Often we have the attitude of "I want it and I want it now!" Our Lord reminds us of the virtue of patience and asks us to wait upon Him.

More strength for steadfastness in our teaching is offered in Acts 2:42: "They joined with the other believers in regular attendance at the apostles' teaching sessions and at the communion services and prayer meetings." Being regular in the enabling of your students is vital. As you continually seek to compliment them, build them up, and find personal ways to minister to each student, you are fulfilling your commission as an affirming teacher.

As a Sunday church school teacher you can meet the needs of your class members by demonstrating a deep commitment. Such persistence motivates members to believe in a power that moves deeper than the surface enthusiasm of a group. This commitment keeps classes strong, even when enthusiasm is low. Persistence involves loyalty to what you know in your head rather than what you might feel one low moment.

3. *I was a stranger and you welcomed me . . .*

Do you accept class members where they are in their walk with God? Instead of being judgmental about behavior and attitudes, you can show students that your concern accepts them as they are.

"Ronnie is so slow," a third grade teacher remarked at a recent teacher's meeting. "Just wait until you get his sister Brenda," the preschool teacher laughed. "She is so active; I'll bet she is hyper!"

Have you ever labeled a student in your class? As parents, there are many moments when we carelessly call one of our children "motor mouth" or "high strung." As insignificant as these labels may seem, nicknames can be devastating for any individual.

Labels are usually developed out of the habit of continually emphasizing only one dominant trait in a person. And while the label may sometimes be positive, usually the remark is derogatory.

One of the greatest hazards in labeling a person in a Sunday church school classroom is that can limit the adult, youth, or child's

God-given potential. A person who is labeled as bossy may always try to live up to that title. Another person who is discussed as being sloppy may never feel incentive to change these habits.

Reflect on your childhood experiences in the Sunday church school. Do you remember having peers who were described as being "uncontrollable" or "too loud"? Perhaps your teacher believed children should be seen and not heard in the Sunday church school classroom. Did you feel comfortable each week? Did you believe you could truly be yourself?

A close friend who is an ordained minister disclosed, "I was always called a mischief maker by my Sunday church school teachers, and I enjoyed living up to that name. When I was called into the ministry, no one believed it was for real. I guess they thought I was kidding, as usual."

We all have the opportunity to change as we develop as Christians. You can encourage your class members to realize their full potential if you refrain from labeling their personalities and help them to build on their strengths.

Consider the following suggestions:

1. *Help students become aware of their strengths and weaknesses.*

Talk openly about uniqueness. Put pictures on the bulletin board of people of all races and clutures. Be sure to affirm God's plan for diversity in creating us as you discuss these pictures in class.

Affirmation games that enable children to feel good about themselves are fun to play in the classroom. "I like myself because . . . " or "I like John because . . ." helps children to see each person as being special.

Oversee all activities in the classroom. Has a clique formed and is the new person excluded? Help people open up their small groups and accept others. Is there a class member who dominates the conversation? Be prepared to bring the introverted student into discussions while quieting the talkative ones.

2. *Encourage slaying of personal "dragons."*

Minor fears can become stumbling blocks for many people. You can help class members transform these stumbling blocks into stepping stones by encouraging their attempts to surmount them.

Paul, a sixth grade student, had a speech impediment and always hesitated to speak in class. His teacher is very sensitive to this and purposely refrains from asking Paul questions that might put him on the spot. One day recently the class was talking about the Holy Land. Paul's uncle, a missionary from our church, had just returned from the area with a wealth of pictures, slides, and treasures. When Paul cautiously raised his hand during the class discussion, Mr. David, the teacher, recognized him quickly.

"Maybe my uncle could come and share his trip with us one Sunday. I mean, if everyone wants to hear about it." Paul stuttered as he spoke and obviously wasn't sure if he should have opened his mouth.

Mr. David immediately affirmed his gesture. "Wonderful, Paul! We'll make plans today."

Mr. David combined immediate affirmation with positive support and helped Paul feel good about taking a step toward conquering his stumbling block.

While discouragement can lower the class member's self-esteem, approval from you, the teacher, can help him to believe in himself. He will feel, "I can do it!" and will risk trying again and again.

3. Avoid comparing class members.

"If only they all were like Melanie." Often we are guilty of wishing this as we gaze upon the quiet, studious child, youth, or adult who is so willing to pay attention and answer the questions. But God's world would be boring if we all were alike!

Learn to accept each person as a unique individual. Dominant traits that disrupt in a group situation can be controlled if you establish a caring relationship with the student. Use these traits to benefit others in the classroom. For example, let the talkative adult lead the small group discussion. A shy child could pass out the story papers each week. An active youth could help take the roll and collection. Rather than letting the trait overwhelm the class, it is much better to work *with* the individual.

4. Help your class members explore their potential.

New members will never risk exposing their feelings if they aren't given the chance. Communication games, crowdbreakers, small group sharing, and a caring environment are all important in helping to "break the ice" for timid individuals.

Tools such as music, painting, clay, crayons, and puppets can be excellent ways to bring out the quiet child or youth. The tools help children risk coming outside of themselves and begin to verbalize hidden feelings and emotions.

Is your Sunday church school classroom an open environment where children, youth, and adults can develop into Christian maturity? Your accepting manner will allow your students to feel, "I am free to be me — *even* in Sunday church school!"

4. *I was naked and you clothed me.*

Do you affirm the worth of each person? We discussed the hazards of labeling students in our classrooms and sometimes it is difficult to find something positive about someone. Yet, knowing that God calls each of us by name and made us in his image helps us to go the extra mile in finding special talent.

People in the Sunday church school are often lonely and insecure. As the teacher, you can build each person up, offer a shoulder to lean on, a hand to grasp, and give much needed encouragement as they seek their full potential. Affirmation from a caring Christian can make life's transitions much smoother.

Give of yourself! Make yourself available to those class members who may need someone to talk to. Ideas such as arriving in the classroom early and staying later than usual may help in making yourself accessible to students. Let them know your door is open.

Touch is also vital in communicating affirmation. A pat on the shoulder, a hug, or a firm handshake often generates a stronger sense of caring and concern than spoken words.

In a recent study at a large northern university, a number of students who checked out books at the university library were given a handshake, a pat on the arm, or other touch by the staff librarians. After leaving the building, each student was questioned about his feelings concerning the school's library. Of the students who had been touched, 100% reported positive feelings. But those who were not touched had either apathetic or negative feelings.

In his ministry, Jesus expressed concern and healed many persons through the use of his hands. When Jesus received little children despite his disciples' objections, "He took them in his arms and blessed them, laying his hands upon them." (Mark 10:16) When Peter's mother-in-law was ill, Jesus "touched her hand, and the fever left her." (Matthew 19:15a)

We visualize our Lord putting his arms around children, lifting up the lame, and embracing those in pain. Not only did he preach love and caring, he demonstrated them. He reached out with gentle, caring hands, touching cold and empty lives with his power.

This nonverbal form of love can be used in the Sunday church school classroom to interact in an affirming way with your students. They may be hiding behind masks or feeling insecure about their place in the group. Your touch can be the security they long for.

You can also go that extra mile in affirming each student by modeling caring. The attitude of "who cares" can destroy the respect in the Sunday church school classroom. The teacher's attitude should be "I care" even when no one else does. As the students observe you making decisions, reaching out with God's love, and being genuine and open, they are making a mental picture of what being a Christian is all about. They will feel good about themselves because you cared enough to help.

5. *I was sick and you visited me . . .*

Do you look beyond the problem to the person? Often when we have class members with personal problems we must look past the turmoil to the "why." Perhaps the person is insecure in decision-making and has made some wrong choices. Maybe the person is a victim of unfortunate circumstances. Someone with problems may be facing a crisis in the family. But you, the teacher, are the key in giving the student understanding, and through that gift, affirming the wholeness and healing Christ offers.

In Mark 14:36 Jesus prayed, "Father . . . Father . . . everything is possible for you. Take away this cup from me. Yet, I want your will, not mine." Paul teaches in Philippians 4:13, "I can do everything God asks me to with the help of Christ who gives me the strength and power."

Our Christian faith is one of hope. Realizing the possibility and promise in our lives is one of the keys to successful Christian living. The teacher of one class at First Church had to rediscover this possibility in her small class.

"I seemed to be stuck with all the discipline problems. I dreaded going to teach each week because of confronting these children. Finally, I realized with God's help that I had to take a different attitude. If I could just see the potential in these problem children, I know I could teach and change their lives," she shared. "After many weeks of positive thinking and positive teaching methods, my classroom situation began to turn around. Some of the most defiant children are the most dedicated today."

Seeing the possibility in each student is exciting. The awesome power of God is limitless if the teachers come with an attitude of anticipation.

The psalmist says, "I will pray morning, noon, and night, pleading aloud with God; and he will hear and answer." (Psalm 55:17)

Prayer does change things. In a Sunday church school class, prayer can unite the members and help give purpose to their lives. At Trinity Church, the teacher of the adult class realized the power of prayer in helping their declining situation. He began each class session with conversational prayer, kept ongoing prayer lists, and spoke openly of the changes God had made in his own life. Other members began to sign up for a prayer vigil, vowing to lift up each member and personal problems in morning, noon and nighttime prayers. And, as the class came together each week and prayed, they felt a true koinonia.

Prayer can be that special communication that enables the members to know of God's love and special grace, even when problems seem unsurmountable.

6. *I was in prison and you came to me.*

"I quit!" These two words spoken by a student in a moment of intense anger, can destroy positive feelings in a church and classroom. We adults know that "quitting" the class when conflict occurs is not the best way to solve the initial problem.

Conflict is defined as a sharp disagreement or opposition of interests or ideas. And whenever people get together, even in a Sunday church school classroom, conflict will occur.

The Bible tells stories of families in conflict. The story of Adam and Eve tells how conflict ended in the loss of one son. Even in the earliest days of the church, people experienced the difficulty of facing conflict and differences. In Romans 12:5 Paul affirmed the unity of Christians even though different in many ways: "We, though many, are one body in Christ." Paul was well aware of the diversity of gifts among Christians. He listed: prophecy, service, teaching, exhortation, giving, acting with mercy. (Romans 12:6-7) Yet, Paul also insisted that the church of Jesus Christ is one whole body. Like the human body it needs different kinds of members — hands, feet, ears, eyes. And so does the unified Sunday church school class.

As teacher, you can help keep your class members unified if you deal with conflict situations constructively.

The first step is to listen fairly. One Sunday church school teacher shared, "I used to blame one boy for causing all the problems in my class. It never failed, as soon as I turned my back, all chaos would break loose and he seemed to be in the middle. One day, I noticed two other children antagonizing him, trying to get him angry. I realized that perhaps he was not so guilty and began to really hear all sides of the argument."

Avoid making judgments before an adult, youth, or child speaks. Even then, try to answer their question with a question, such as: "How would you feel? What would you do?" This helps to keep you in the position of mediator and helps the others grow from the conflict as they seek compromise.

Another important rule in keeping conflict positive is to "agree to disagree." Rob, a youth teacher, set the tone with his large class. "Before we begin our discussion, I want to ask that we let people express their opinions openly. This is not to say that you must agree, or that you even have to accept the statements as truth. But we do need to feel enough love and caring for openness to occur."

An adult class member in a small class admitted, "No, I don't agree with what everyone says. But we are all entitled to an opinion, a viewpoint. As we listen, we can learn. And, with God's grace expressed throughout the class, we can pray that we find truth in our own lives."

The third step in solving conflicts is to use creative problem solving in the classroom. The following diagram may help:

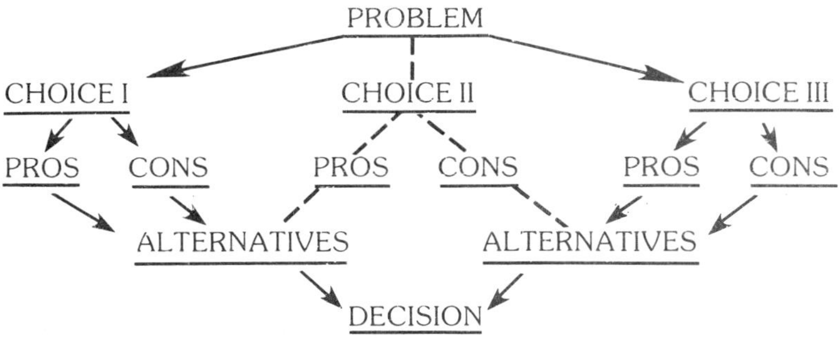

1. Identify the problem in the classroom.
2. Ask: What are the choices that could solve this problem?
3. Ask: Why would this choice be good?
4. Ask: Why would the choice be bad?
5. Consider: Are there other alternatives?
6. Decide: Which decision will you make?

Helping your class members use this thought process as they make even the smallest choices (such as, for example, which new curriculum to use) will increase their awareness of how to make fair decisions.

As committed Christians, we hold a key to freedom through Christ Jesus from the enslavement and conflict that so many of our class members experience. With this key, our students can feel the power and hope that Christ brings to persons' lives. Yet, only through the message of salvation can this conflict and bondage be broken. As committed teachers, we can use those precious times during class study or worship to listen to the problems of our students and offer the strength of the Scriptures. We can help release them into a life of hope and freedom as we encourage, affirm, and enable them to become their best.

Chapter Three

RECREATION
More Than Child's Play

When our close friend Henry retired last year, he found he did not know how to have fun. "I had worked so hard at making a living for fifty years that I never bothered to learn how to recreate," he commented matter-of-factly at a gathering. "Now I just sit at home and watch television. I'd like to play golf or fish with my friends, but I just don't know where to begin. I even think I might feel guilty."

On the other hand, when another friend, Tom, retired recently his entire life broadened. "I had planned for this," Tom said enthusiastically. "I bought a boat a few years ago and joined a sailing club nearby. I look forward to meeting with my friends each weekend to learn more about the sport."

A lot of driven individuals criticize their relaxed friends who spend weekends on the golf course, bowling with a league, or having get-togethers with acquaintances. "A waste of time," one workaholic friend declares. "Your life should always accomplish goals and if you are playing, then you are just not doing that."

Yet, recreation, play, and fellowship with others are vital to human beings as people replenish the creativity that is often lost in the work week. Play is also important as individuals learn how to put into practice what they have learned about the Christian lifestyle. Attributes such as cooperation, caring, and sharing are all vital in playing with others. And families and friends can celebrate closeness as they make time to recreate together.

But what about recreation in the local church? Do play and fellowship activities have a vital place in the balanced Sunday school program?

A group of concerned parents from First Church met with the Director of Christian Education after the evening youth program. The problem? Recreation.

"When I was growing up the church represented strict values and Biblical teaching," one mother shared. "Now my children come to the youth group because they want to have fun with their friends and play volleyball."

"I know what you mean," another father said. "I want my son to be taught values, not just to play."

Another group of church members complained of similar feelings. At Asbury Church, the adult class took pride in their successful and well-attended monthly pot-luck dinners. Yet, some of the members questioned the validity of such. "Should we really be enjoying ourselves so much?" a serious class member asked. "Aren't we here primarily to study and learn?"

A lot of well-meaning church members criticize or neglect the use of recreation and fellowship in the Sunday church school program. Most feel that the time at church should be spent entirely in Bible study and serious discussions. Yet, recreation is a vital part of the church's ministry as members engage in Christian fellowship. People learn how to put into practice what they have been taught about the Christian way of life. This is not to say that a Sunday church school class period should be spent entirely in fellowship or play. Rather, recreation can be beneficial in a gathering or party in enabling members to get better acquainted and in celebrating the fellowship that is within the group.

Let's look at the life of our Lord. Jesus gives many examples that further explain the need for Christian fellowship. Remember the wedding feast in Cana that Jesus celebrated with family and friends? The meal in Bethany at the home of Lazarus was a true gathering of close friends in fellowship. In fact, Jesus spent much of his ministry talking with people in their homes. At one point he was accused falsely of being "a gluttonous man and wine bibber." (Matthew 11:16-19) This caring habit of being with the people and sharing refreshment together carried on into the early Christian church where "fellowship" played a big part of the ministry — "Breaking bread from house to house." (Acts 2:46)

Recreation or fellowship today is defined as any form of play, amusement, or relaxation used for refreshment. Psychologists have long recognized the need for play among young developing children in order for them to fully experience their environment. And in the local church's Sunday church school, most educators and teachers agree with this theory and allow ample time for children to learn Biblical teachings through interaction and play. But in recent years, studies have also shown that play is important for older people too. Reports that teens and adults can lower stress levels with the proper use of relaxation and leisure time have encouraged people to make time to recreate.

Play uses every ounce of a child's (or youth's and adult's) energy. It stimulates the imagination. It develops skill of both body and mind. It brings about understanding, warmth, and sympathy toward others.

How to compete, how to take hard knocks, how to win gracefully, when to assert oneself, and when to forget self-interest are all learned through play. Perseverance — how to struggle through to a desired end — is as much a part of play as it is of work.

Play offers healing for hurts and sadness. It breaks down tension and releases pent-up urges toward self-expression. Play is the working partner for growth, for activity is as vital to growth as food and sleep."[1]

Play and recreation refer to anything that re-creates, makes new, or adds life. In the Sunday church school class, this recreation can refer to fellowship times, activities that are light and carefree, or times of play and leisure.

But why is Christian recreation important? Must a successful Sunday church school program incorporate times of play?

Just as a balanced diet helps develop a healthy person, a balanced life contributes to maximum personal development. Such a balance includes a variety of refreshing or renewing activities — a fellowship of enjoyment.

Activities entered into in the spirit of recreation — being made new while having fun — are fellowship builders. Through recreation at its best, persons are affirmed, skills are developed, and relationships are strengthened. This play provides another way of learning interesting facts and constructive attributes and can contribute to personal enrichment.[2]

Christian recreation used in the Sunday church school program helps to minister to the whole person, creating an educational balance.

1. *Spiritual* — Christian ideals that are put into every phase of ministry become a foundation for spiritual growth.

2. *Mental* — Deeper and more meaningful Christian principles should be taught and applied to life as people mature mentally.

3. *Social* — Strong friendships, built on a foundation of individual love and acceptance, are invaluable to ministry.

4. *Emotional* — Understanding and accepting self is a major facet of emotional maturity. Recreational experiences are actual life situations where this understanding can begin to take place.

5. *Physical* — Activity and action are by-words of people today.[3]

When members in a Sunday church school class take time to recreate and play together, they can make new discoveries about self and others. This fellowship is vital for personal and group growth. Regular times of recreation and togetherness offer class members a chance to develop a sense of belonging — aside from the hurried hour on Sunday morning. Members can share personal hobbies and talents as they engage in casual small talk. People can find special abilities that would never surface in a classroom as they play games together. And recreation on a regular basis can take the stuffiness out of the Christian faith as the ice is broken. Then, real growth occurs as people feel comfortable in confiding in friends their own sufferings, concerns, goals, and joys.

This friendship developed through fellowship times is a sign of Sunday church school success. "Most successful Sunday church school classes are more than just a group of people who want to study the faith together. Research has shown that in many classes a significant percentage of the member's best personal friends are also members of that class (*The Parish Paper*, Yokefellow Institute, March, 1974, Lyle E. Schaller, ed.). In fact, it is through the life of the class that their friendships ripen into lasting bonds.[4]

Recreation Opportunities

The opportunities for play and recreation in the Sunday church school are limitless, depending on how creative you and your members are. The following list comprises just a few main categories that classes have found useful in expanding their fellowship opportunities.

A. CROWDBREAKERS — Often called "icebreakers," these are activities used to help groups relax, laugh, and begin to break down communication barriers. In doing so, the members usually become more responsive to the material or lesson that follows. Instead of worrying about the person next to them, the members can tune-in to the leader with a relaxed feeling. Thus, learning can take place.

Crowdbreakers can be as simple as a time for telling names and occupations or hobbies before the lesson, or more complicated planned activities that encourage interaction among members. A common game used for crowdbreakers is "the attributes game": each person identifies a color, animal, or shape they feel akin to. Other ideas for crowdbreakers useful in a Sunday church school setting can be found in recreational books at Christian bookstores.

B. CLASS SOCIALS — Socials are outings, usually after class time, where members can meet on an informal basis. Members of the same class may never know one another's names. Socials help to draw these members together and encourage communication with the use of games, crowdbreakers, and relaxed mingling. A social is an excellent time to include new, interested prospects who may feel insecure in attending on Sunday morning.

C. DINNERS — The importance of "breaking bread" is written throughout the history of the Christian church. A common meal — such as communion or a Love Feast at Easter, or a dinner on the grounds — has always been important. Dinners can be of the "pot-luck" type, to which members bring their special recipe. Or they can be seasonal, complete with table decorations and costumes. Holidays provide regular occasions for celebration, food, and fellowship. Christmas caroling with turkey dinner, a Halloween hot dog roast and hay ride for the youth, a Saint Patrick's Day progressive dinner, or a Valentine's Day candlelight dinner for adults are just a few suggestions.

D. MUSIC AND SING-ALONGS — Music "just for fun" is another form of recreation that is popular in Sunday church school classes. Old-fashioned hymn sings, creating contemporary words to fit the old tunes, and having a homemade rhythm band performance can be fun for classes of all ages.

Some successful Sunday church school programs have inter-generational assemblies where members of all ages meet before class to sing, share their joys and concerns, and get to know one another. Music plays a vital role for increasing participation and creating a mood of fun and pleasure in such assemblies.

E. GAMES — Contests can be used for teaching a skill, or just for having fun. Games can also be non-competitive. Teachers in the early grades might find games useful in channeling some of the extra energy among students. Youth teachers could use simulation games to help young people feel what an experience is really like, such as pretending to be hungry in a poverty country and making decisions how to provide food for a starving family. Adult teachers might not use the games in the classroom, but choose rather a social event such as "game night".

F. SPORTS — Here can be fun for all ages. Softball teams, volleyball games, basketball tournaments, bowling leagues, and the like are forms of active recreation for men and women in the local church. Sports events allow church members to experience an ecumenical gathering as they play teams from various denominations. These active forms of recreation are good for the "sideline" class member who doesn't want to commit to Sunday morning, but still desires fellowship with other Christians.

G. RETREATS AND CAMPING — The word *retreat* means to go back, to withdraw to a safe or private place. The world spins faster and faster around us. A retreat can provide that time of quiet to hear that "still small voice" of God. Retreats allow members in a Sunday church school class time to be alone and to reflect on the past experience and knowledge they have gained. Retreats also may be useful for setting personal goals and class goals for the upcoming season. Some adult classes include family members from time to time while others like to keep the intimacy of the group at the retreat.

Planning is the Key!

Whether you are preparing for a class social, a sports event, or even a crowdbreaker on Sunday morning, the toal success in your recreation or fellowship times depends on the planning you initiate.

Planning Games

Educators claim that 60% of our learning occurs when we are actually "doing" or participating in the learning activity. The information becomes real as we experience the situation and are involved in some form of the decision-making process. Not only do we internalize the problem, but we are able to participate in making choices for a successful outcome.

By using indoor games in a classroom situation, we can offer students an opportunity to get involved actively in the learning process. Not only do games get the attention of the entire group, but the fast pace and excitement usually keep the interest of even the most active child. And, if the Sunday church school teacher uses both foresight and hindsight, even the shyest person who hesitates to speak can become a vital part of the classroom experience.

Perhaps the following suggestions can help Sunday church school teachers develop a process for using indoor games creatively and effectively in the classroom.

1. Set the Goal for the Activity.

What message do you hope to convey to the group? In a preschool class, perhaps the goal is to understand taking turns. An elementary class might be involved in problem solving such as trying to find a Bible person from a list of given clues. And a youth class may have to compile facts from various learning centers to reach a conclusion on a subject such as "Solutions for World Hunger." Whatever the activity, be sure that you have a definite goal set for the class, in case the game becomes mere action and little or no learning.

One Sunday church school teacher found that by placing a large poster with the goal printed on it and periodically asking the group if the goal was still being sought, that the outcome generally became a learning experience. Another teacher of youth had her class establish its own goals for the game, helping them to feel ownership in the activity and in the projected results. No matter how it is stated, be sure the outcome meets the initial goal. Or, if the goal is not met, be sure the class discusses reasons why.

2. Be Prepared.

Carefully plan the activity ahead of time taking into consideration the maturity level of the students, amount of time and space, and the idea you want to convey through the game. Use the week before the class time to obtain the necessary supplies, timers, markers, or any other items needed for the activity. Allow adequate time in the structured period to play the game, with extra time set aside for questions, evaluation, and discussion.

Be sure that you completely understand the game and have experimented with the instructions before you approach the students. Not all games are geared for the inside classroom and not all games written are fun. Select the game that meets your particular needs.

3. Be Specific.

Make sure that your students understand the directions. This involves being specific, outlining procedures for playing fairly, and allowing time for questions. If there is confusion, give a sample demonstration of how the game is to be played. Don't take for granted that, just because the instructions were given, all students were listening and have understood. Ask for feedback from the group. Quesions could be asked such as "Did you understand that move in the game," or "What would you do if that occurred during the game." Feel confident that all participants know the rules before starting the procedure.

4. All Are Winners.

Scores are unimportant in Christian recreation and games. What is important is that all players become sensitive to one another, play fairly, and share in the fellowship of the group. Ask: "Did everyone receive an equal chance at the game?" "Was anyone left out of the activity?" "Did one person hoard the game?" It is the duty of the classroom teacher to act as an overseer in making sure that the rules are being followed, that no one is left out, and that each student has an equal turn.

If teams are used in the game, select a creative method of dividing up the class. There is nothing worse for a child than being chosen last to participate on a team. Ideas such as numbering the students 1, 2, 3, 4, and having all like numbers line up at a certain spot can be used without isolating certain children. Or labeling the children wtih animal names such as dog, cat, and mouse, and then letting them find their team by making the animal's sound has been used successfully with all ages and helps to break the competitive barrier.

5. Evaluate and Teach.

During the course of the game, find time to insert ideas relating to the projected objective. Ask questions or suggest insights to help the students get on the right track to finding the answer or goal. In a pre-school class a teacher could say "How does it feel when you don't get a turn?" A teacher might suggest that the team repeat the procedure if there is a question in making the game's goal. Bring out the pertinent points relating to the goal to assure that learning will take place.

After the game is over, ask the students if they enjoyed participating in the activity as opposed to being "told" the information. Receive feedback and suggestions that could make the next game more productive. Question your own instruction. Ask yourself: Did the students understand the game? Did I have enough props? enough time? Was the outcome what I intended or were new insights established? Evaluation allows for growth, and, if used in a positive manner, should broaden horizons for the group.

Games can make learning a pleasant experience. Indoor games, especially used during the winter months, give a much needed break from the routine of sitting, listening, and talking. Games can especially benefit the group as people begin interacting with one another, facades break down, and the real person is disclosed. The teacher is able to communicate "I love you just because you are you" in a way that could well become stifled in a quiet lecture setting. And, most important, the Christian faith can be taught and understood as one of joy and celebration as students participate actively in an exciting learning experience.

Planning Socials

Planning class socials and parties also takes careful preparation and is just as important as planning for class lessons.

1. Choose Persons to Handle the Details.

You might elect a social chairperson to be in charge of the details for socials. This person may work alone or with a committee and needs to be responsible for setting the location, the date, the attire, the theme, the food, etc. The social committee should also give advance publicity to class members at least two weeks before the social or party. Letters in the mail, the church bulletin, word of mouth, and (perhaps most important) personal phone calls are all important ways of communicating the message.

2. Plan Regular Fellowship Times.

The Sunday church school classes whose members are discovering friendships among one another are those who "recreate" together on a regular basis. Many groups have found that monthly socials, outings, service projects, or retreats have helped to increase attendance during the class time. Persons begin to like one another because they get to know one another, which is often difficult to do on Sunday morning during a lesson.

3. Invite New Persons to the Social Event.

Don't let your class parties become "inclusive" affairs. Rather, constantly reach out to unchurched friends, visitors, and interested newcomers and *bring* them to the class functions. New people may feel more comfortable coming first to a social, *then* to the Sunday morning class.

Remember to include other persons who cannot attend the class on Sunday morning. Teachers, education leaders, the pastor and family, and others who are busy leading the Sunday church school program are often forgotten at class socials. This monthly get-together helps them to have a support group of Christians.

4. Use the Social Wisely.

The fellowship time is the perfect time to get to know one another. But members must make an effort to mingle, meet new people, and build relationships. If class members stay with their same friends each time, the purpose can be lost. Be sure to plan crowdbreakers and recreational games to help break the ice so that communication takes place. Some classes assign various members to serve as greeters for the gathering, just to make sure that people don't get "too comfortable" in meeting new friends.

Class socials can add special benefits to any Sunday church school class. One very strong adult class in the Midwest had in its yearbook a firm policy: "Social meetings — Third Friday night of the month at 6:30 with a covered dish dinner, unless otherwise specified. Fellowship Hall has been reserved for these meetings." (*The Brownie Sunday School Class Yearbook*, 1972-73, Des Moines, Iowa) This was kept up for over fifty years, and now that the class has discontinued meeting on Sunday morning, occasional social events continue. Most members are now in their eighties.[5]

Socials can help make Sunday church school more than just a place to learn on Sunday morning. In fact, regular recreation and fellowship times can help the members realize true koinonia in the group.

Planning Class Retreats

Retreats help members to put their faith into practice. A weekend of living together, playing together, and expressing new ideas and feelings can be comparable to a dozen classes in a Sunday church school classroom.

Retreats should include several elements — education, worship, fellowship and recreation, service, dedication. Some retreats deliberately emphasize some elements more than others, depending on the goals set by group members.

In planning for a class retreat, these details will need attention:

1. Date — Time — Publicity
2. Place — Costs, deposit
3. Theme — Speaker or Resources
4. Activities — Schedule
5. Budget — Food, games, supplies

You may choose to assign different committees to head up each category in planning for a class retreat.

Depending on the size of the retreat group, you may choose creative ways to handle the theme for the weekend. Some classes broaden the theme with the use of name tags, appropriate games, crafts, and appropriate crowdbreakers.

Be sure to choose a retreat site and date that is best suited for all members. If most of the class members camp, then look into the denomination's campgrounds or national parks. If you want a "weekend off" from cooking, make sure the campgrounds provide meals for retreats.

All resources you need for the weekend must be brought with the group — Bibles, paper, pencils, flashlights, rain gear, etc. Make sure the class members are thorough in gathering the necessary items for the weekend.

Schedules are important, even for retreats, for they help members to have a well-rounded weekend. The following retreat schedule offers a workable way your class can benefit from a weekend or overnight together.

How about it? Why not plan some recreation for your Sunday church school class? Combined with careful planning, goal setting, low-key competition, and mingling with fellow Christians, recreation can be that special time where relationships can begin and friendships can be the result.

Recreation can be a time of re-creation in your class when barriers are diminished and an awareness of others takes place. No wonder it's been said that "groups that play together stay together!"

Weekend Prayer Retreat

(Plan to arrive in time to unload your gear before the evening meal.)

6:00 P.M.	Supper and chores
7:00	Orientation and group building
8:00	Organize into small prayer groups (to be used also for meal preparation and clean-up duties)
8:15	Prayer group sharing
9:00	Break to settle in and organize supplies
9:30	Presentation on prayer and meditation; guided meditation
10:00	Prayer groups — reflecting, beginning prayer journals
10:45	Snacks and informal activity
11:30	Quiet Time
Midnight	Curfew — lights out
7:30 A.M.	Morning Prayers
8:00	Breakfast and chores
9:00	Group session on prayers — biblical, classical, and contemporary prayers
10:00	Prayer groups — spontaneous prayers, reflections
11:00	Planned recreation
Noon	Lunch and chores
1:00 P.M.	Time alone for personal meditation and prayer journals
2:00	Interest groups on *visual prayers* — dance, banner making, poster making
4:00	Free time
6:00	Evening prayers
6:30	Supper and chores
7:30	Group session on *songs of prayer* — traditional hymns and contemporary songs
8:30	Prayer groups
9:30	Service of prayer and meditation
10:45	Snacks and informal activity
11:30	Quiet time
Midnight	Curfew — lights out
7:30 A.M.	Morning prayers
8:00	Breakfast and chores
9:00	Group session on *works of prayer* — lives of the saints
10:00	Prayer groups — prayers for persons in group, plan for continuing prayer life, reflections on retreat
11:00	Time for individual prayer journals and reflection
Noon	Lunch and chores
1:00 P.M.	Service of commitment
1:30	Packing and clean-up
2:00	On the road

Overnight Recreation Retreat

11:30 A.M.	Move in
Noon	Eat
1:00 P.M.	Get-acquainted games
2:30	Study of competition vs. cooperation
3:30	Free time for nonstructured recreation — frisbees, swimming, and so forth
5:30	Eat and do chores
7:00	Small groups: create your own games, indoor recreation, games for small spaces
9:00	Folk dancing, musical games
10:30	Closing worship
Midnight	Curfew — lights out
7:30 A.M.	Breakfast and chores
8:30	Time for personal recreation
9:00	Study of inclusion vs. exclusion
10:00	Outdoor hike, trust walk
11:30	Clean up site, load cars
Noon	Eat
12:45 P.M.	Worship/celebration
1:30	On the road

Bibliography

1. *Your Child From 6 to 12.* (US Department of Health, Education, and Welfare, 1949). Publication.
2. *UMYF Handbook* (Prepared by the Youth Ministry Staff, Board of Discipleship, Nashville, 1980). p. 15.
3. *The Complete Youth Ministries Handbook,* (J. David Stone, editor, Creative Youth Ministries Models, Louisiana, 1979). p. 196.
4. *Strengthening the Adult Sunday School Class.* (Dick Murray, Creative Leadership Series, Abingdon, Nashville, 1981). p. 67.
5. *Strengthening the Adult Sunday School Class,* p. 68.
6. Retreat Schedule from *Youth Leader,* Spring 1982. United Methodist Church, Board of Discipleship, Frances Brooks, Ed. Article "*Retreat Together*" by Jeanette Fagerberg and Debra F. Bruce.

Chapter Four

EDUCATION
The Role of The Teacher

Janet Hill, a full-time homemaker and mother of two preschoolers, teaches the large adult Sunday church school class at Pine Ridge Church.

Dr. Ralph Benton, a professor at a northwestern university and single parent, teaches the 5th and 6th grade at Christ Church.

Don and Evelyn Southerland, a retired military couple, teach the preschool class at Beach's Church.

Rev. Martha Quinten, a diaconal minister on leave of absence, teaches the youth at East Church.

Who can be educators in Christ's church? Anyone can! As long as they are open to God's spirit, responsive to the personal needs of class members, and continually enabling others to experience God's grace.

Many church school superintendents, pastors, and leaders in education try to find the most "trained" laypersons to teach Sunday church school classes. Yet, those Sunday church school programs which are experiencing success, both quantitatively and qualitatively, are using laypeople who do not necessarily have teaching backgrounds. Instead, these teachers of the Word of God are all ages, from all walks of life, and have many unique talents, but with one thing in common — an ability to teach in such a way that others experience — and are confronted with — God's grace.

This grace can be experienced through watching a sunset at the seashore, in the eyes of an innocent child, through comfort in times of tragedy, and can be shared by you in the Sunday church school classroom. And to those who experience love through grace, faith in God is the intended result.

But what is faith? Can faith be taught in the Sunday church school classroom?

Faith means commitment, trust, caring for others. Faith enables us to risk sharing our lives with others in meaningful relationships. Because of faith that is nurtured in a caring Sunday church school classroom, new lives are constantly being changed. And faith in a living Lord gives empty, lonely lives new meaning and purpose.

Faith is an ongoing process. Theologians realize that just as people mature and grow in stages, so do we develop in stages with our faith, especially as our faith matures. Religious educators have found that just as a baby crawls before he walks and develops physically and mentally in sequence, so does our Christian faith in God.

In the book *Will Our Children Have Faith?* author John Westerhoff, III, suggests four stages of faith development.[1]

1. Experienced faith – In this beginning stage, the person believes only what is experienced. Other people are observed and copied. This experience stage is highlighted by action and reaction towards others and events.

2. Affiliative faith – The person moves into affiliating with significant persons and events. Affiliative faith involves belonging, such as to a group, participation, and a feeling of being part of something important.

3. Searching faith – The person begins to use his/her mind to make critical judgments, including questioning and doubting. The person also begins to experiment with alternative courses of action.

4. *Owned faith* – This is the ultimate ideal. Faith is truly "owned." The person begins to feel the need to witness, to behave with an integrity which supports what is believed.

Most educators see their task in the local church's Sunday church school as a "teacher" of the Good News. Yet developing one's personal faith in God is another added and necessary challenge. We can offer experiences to help students move from one faith stage to another as we encourage relationships in the classroom — between teacher and student, student and student, and, especially, between student and God. In fact, before any sharing of information a teacher should first ensure that the classroom environment is conducive for growth. Once this setting is appropriate, the teacher can then allow for prayer, begin sharing, and affirm each person with God's grace and caring. This, again, involves a risk on your part as you reveal your own inner needs, your goals, and your set-backs. It gives you a chance to minister to students, and they to you. It provides time for you to affirm them, listening to their personal struggles, and affectionately building them up as children of God.

The teacher must allow room for personal learning in the classroom. Education is as significant as its relationships. More important than methods and materials of learning are the persons (teachers and pupils) who learn together. If teachers are not learning, either assuming they have learned enough or by preferring other times and situations for learning, there is little possibility for the pupil to learn either. The indifferent teacher creates no interest in the subject, and if it does not fire his enthusiasm, why should it arouse a response in the pupil?[2]

Rather than merely disseminating information, the successful Sunday church school teacher must try to make a difference by relating the Bible to real life situations. The classroom teacher must always be alert to the question, "Can my students grow from what I am teaching them?"

Candy, a teacher and leader of a growing young adult class, was confronted with this challenge. "I chose a very contemporary study trying to appeal to the young adults in our congregation," she said. "This hit upon topics such as separation, anxiety, and relationships.

Yet, it was not Biblical, merely the opinion of the author. I realized that we had too many questions and too few answers, so the class voted to begin a real Bible study in the class. Although the material we had studied was excellent for mature Christians, for our class it was not meeting life needs."

People are what matter in teaching today. Persons are more important than the information to be learned or the way of teaching that is used. Any factual information is useless unless it is of value to the individual and makes a difference in his life. Information should be used to assist the individual to become more mature, not to enslave him with an accumulation of many unrelated, unmeaningful facts.[3]

Jesus said "Where two or three are gathered in my name, there am I in the midst of them." (Matthew 18:20) Is the spirit of the Lord alive in your classroom? In your personal life? Teaching was the most characteristic activity of Jesus during his earthly ministry. He proclaimed the Kingdom of God, called individuals to repentance, and invited them to come to him in faith. But he did all of this primarily through teaching. More often than not, teaching was the vehicle for his proclaimation of the gospel of the kingdom. He taught in synagogues, in the Temple, in private homes, and in wayside places. Much of his teaching was devoted to developing his disciples as Kingdom men. But his teaching also had an evangelistic thrust, for it was designed to bring individuals into the kingdom.[4]

It is the challenge of the Sunday church school teacher not only to share information, but to teach for a gracious confrontation — providing that environment where grace can be experienced and faith can develop.

Planning — The First Step

Once you feel comfortable in "teaching to change lives" you need constantly to brush up on practical methods that can enhance your planning and communication skills.

One of the most common complaints from Sunday church school teachers across the country is, "I don't have time to look at the lesson during the week." And, the usual response from editors of curriculum is "Well, then you just don't have time to teach!"

Rule number one: Teaching takes time, and *planning* is the first step. Reviewing your curriculum weekly, setting teaching goals, and becoming familiar with Scripture passages are essential for effective Sunday church school teaching. In addition, the conscientious teacher must make time to review and study before the class period.

Here are some suggestions to help make planning easier:

1. Develop a habit.

Each week, choose the same time to review the curriculum. This may be the Sunday night before or the weekend before the lesson is to be taught. Find a comfortable chair in a quiet room and gather all materials you will need — Bible, pencils, paper, curriculum, and other commentaries.

2. Read the material.

Believe it or not, many excellent teachers do not even read the material. Instead, they skim for the main idea and begin to prepare to teach. This may work for the "experts," but most of us need to read carefully what the author is saying, underline the main points, and mark ideas in question.

Write down, in your own words, the main idea of the unit you are to teach. Under this main idea, write down specific points that help to support this idea.

3. Plan for your class.

Once you become familiar with the material you are to teach, think of your particular class and their unique needs. Ask: How can I make this lesson relevant to my class? Are there specific life and faith needs to which this lesson speaks? Look at the writer's suggestions for ways to present the material. Would these be met with enthusiasm in your class? Jot down other ideas that you have found useful in teaching that may pertain to the topic. Plot your way through the session and see if you receive the desired outcome. Will the main purpose of the session be served if you teach according to what you have written on your planbook?

4. Study details.

Review charts, maps, pictures, and other teaching aids that are suggested. Will these enhance learning in your class? Try to understand what is taking place in each before you use these in your actual teaching.

Look up the Scripture references in various commentaries. Do you understand the meaning of each? Are there other Scriptures that would be useful to the lesson? Write these down for classroom use.

5. Put it together.

Summarize and organize your class session. Organize your pages in the order in which you intend to teach the material. Have other resources, commentaries, and teaching aids ready with the curriculum material for Sunday morning use. And keep the lesson in your thoughts and prayers throughout the week as you look for ways God speaks on this particular topic.

At a recent church school workshop, Bishop Earl Hunt, serving the Florida Annual Conference of the United Methodist Church, stated emphatically that the Sunday church school is the hope of the church for the 1980's.

Bishop Hunt challenged all laypersons, teachers, and leaders to become creative in their thinking and enthusiastic in relating curriculum and the message of the gospels to their classes.

Educators tell us that learning results when enthusiastic teachers involve class members in personal situations. Thus, creative methods, teaching aids, and other innovative helps are vital in the classroom today in order to "teach for a gospel confrontation."

Methods — The Second Step

Small groups may be useful in many ways in the church school setting. Here are some ideas you may use in your classroom.

1. Small Group Discussion.

A small group discussion is beneficial for timid students: they are free to risk opening themselves with two or three others, rather than riskier sharing in a large group. A small group is especially good for "internalizing" the subject as students ask "How does this relate to my own life?"

2. Buzz Groups.

Three or four individuals gather to share opinions and then report to the larger group. Often one person is selected to be the spokesperson from the group after information is gathered.

3. Research.

A problem is given to the group and the members must research and report the answer. This could involve using the Bible to find supportive Scriptures or going to the church library to find answers in various commentaries. The main advantage is that the students must do the searching for information.

4. Project Groups.

The class members work jointly on a group project such as a service venture or a scrapbook of class events. This group usually meets for several weeks or until the project is completed.

5. Creative Dramatics.

Methods such as role play, mime or mini-drama are useful in creative teaching. Using one of these methods, a problem could be acted out or a situation described. Always be sure the class is involved in analyzing the situation and plotting the best outcome.

6. Crafts.

Arts and crafts are another way of making a lesson come alive. Making murals, mobiles, scrapbooks, collages, bulletin boards, banners, and the like are fun ways of "doing" while learning.

7. Creative writing.

This method can be used as a response to a taught lesson. Students may write a creed expressing their faith, prayers, songs, poems, or other. This method is especially useful with older youth or young adults who may not enjoy arts and crafts.

When using creative methods to teach the class session, you must remember to relate to the entire group. Some ways to increase group effectiveness include:

1. State the goal clearly.

What are you trying to accomplish with the method? You may write the goal on a blackboard and have group members refer to this periodically as they do research, writing, or crafts.

2. Outline the method process.

Tell the group members a way of doing the method. Instead of merely saying "Find this answer," suggest "You might find the answer by searching in this book" and state the specific book. This provides group members a place to begin the search for information and helps them avoid wasting valuable time looking for direction.

3. Encourage evaluation among group members.

Suggest that the group evaluate their answers before sharing with the large group. Evaluation helps members see if they have met the specific goal and if all members have participated in the project. Be sure to keep the evaluation positive and focused on the project, not on the participating members.

4. *Encourage sharing with the large group.*

Always state there are no wrong answers when group members begin to share. The Sunday church school classroom should be that one caring group where feelings, ideas, and opinions can be verbalized without fear of criticism. It is the teacher's duty to keep this atmosphere nonjudgmental.

Storytelling is a method that most teachers in children's classrooms use each week. Yet, have you ever told a story to your students and found yourself getting lost in the body of the material? Or perhaps you forgot the climax, the whole reason for telling the tale.

Storytelling is one of the oldest tools for communicating a message. Jesus used parables — stories with a message — to teach the crowds. In our own families we learn of our heritage from listening to stories handed down through the generations. In fact, the favorite phrase at bedtime in most households with young children is, "Please tell me a story."

Using stories to communicate God's Word and the message of salvation to children and youth in the Sunday church school classroom can be extremely effective. The students can relate to a character in the story or to the predicament in which a character may find himself. Interest is aroused as the students hear a vivid background description and get involved in the developing plot.

Telling stories in the classroom, however, isn't as easy as it may seem. Perhaps the following suggestions will help you to share God's message through stories without losing your class's attention.

1. *Know your story.*

You need not memorize the story word for word, but a good storyteller studies and understands thoroughly the message of the account. It is important to have a clear understanding of the characters involved — their names, their personalities, and their relationships with one another. It is also vital to understand the plot and how the various segments of the story feed into this plot.

Before presenting the story to your class, take time to ask, "Who is the leading character? What are his dominant characteristics? What obstacle is she facing? How does he or she overcome this? Who else is involved?" The more aware you become of the facts you are going to present, the better your class will understand the entire message.

2. *Know your characters.*

What are the characters all about? If the story is a Biblical account, a trip to the library could help you identify their personalities more clearly. Find out the duties of the people during that time and their social status. Were girls allowed to be outspoken as was the character in the story? Does this make the character more unique? The more information you find on the historical background, the better equipped you will be to identify the true characteristics of the people involved.

3. *Know the main points.*

Some people become terrified at the very thought of having to tell a story without a book at hand. If this is the case, outline the main ideas on 3 x 5 inch index cards. Use this outline to remind you of important movements in the story, names of people and places, or Scripture passages that are relevant to the plot.

4. *Be creative.*

Use props if necessary. A modern day story about young John's having to share his new skateboard with his best friend comes alive as you bring a skateboard to show the class. Or a story that takes place in the days of the early Christians becomes more real as you don the garb of that day. One teacher in our Sunday church school department brought a variety of New Testament foods for the younger elementary students to sample — figs, olives, fruits. This helped to make the message more real to the children.

Use practice and expression to enhance your storytelling ability. It has been said that "practice makes perfect." In storytelling, practice will help you to feel more at ease when sharing the message. As you repeat the words over and over, you will become secure with the material. Once you are able to tell the story comfortably to a small audience, such as members of your family, try using expression and voice fluctuation to create interest and excitement.

Ask questions to involve every class member. Include such questions as: Have you ever felt this way? Did you want something very badly as Susan did? The class's response will encourage you to continue. And the questions help to involve the students personally in the story. Including them in the storytime will hold their attention to the end.

Interject your own experiences. Have you had an experience similar to the one with which the main character is struggling? Perhaps the experience was very recent. Share your own struggles and how you solved them with God's help. The story will become real as you identify wtih the conflict involved. By sharing your own personal adventures, you are helping to deepen your relationship with the students in the class.

Storytelling is an important tool in sharing God's Word. As you prepare your next story, you can use these suggestions to become a proficient storyteller — one who can excite and involve your students and help them make decisions in their lives.

Discussion is another useful teaching tool with all ages. But using discussion with children and youth can sometimes be very frustrating. Have you ever tried discussing with children or youth in your Sunday church school class, only to receive blank stares? Or perhaps their replies were simply "yes" or "no," rather than a thoughtful reply.

Having a discussion with children or youth about a specific topic, idea, or Scripture verse can be difficult. Often the subject matter is not geared to their level of thinking. Sometimes the problem stems from the way the question is worded. Even the teacher may feel unsure as to how to continue the discussion once it begins.

Yet an active discussion of a Bible verse or an idea from the Sunday church school lesson can be a tremendous experience for both teacher and child. Feelings can be exposed, new insight will be gained, and personal growth can occur as communication takes place. In an active discussion the children can experience the topic. They can relate it to their own lives, and the Scripture verse or idea becomes internalized. They can discover new meaning and personal awareness as they think through the topic presented.

Perhaps the following "dos and don'ts" will offer you insight in how to lead a discussion with children and youth.

Do know the age group you are teaching. Ask "Can the child of this age think abstractly?" and "Does this question relate to their social development?" Often questions are over the children's heads. Biblical terms, such as "light" and "magnify" are often taken literally by younger children.

In order to understand the age group you teach, you must read books that describe specific developmental traits. Talk with other teachers in the church who have insight into the specific age and observe the unique qualities of the children in your class.

One teacher explains that she asked the children what some signs of God's love were. A preschooler answered, "A stop sign and an exit sign." The word *sign* had a completely different meaning for the adult and the child (although a quick-witted teacher could have made good use of this youngster's unusual response). Thoughts and feelings will come alive if you use vocabulary that is understood by the age group.

Don't mold the children into your way of thinking. Accept what they have to say and thank them. Some children and youth (and some adults!) express a simple theology that is not like yours. Still, the children's thoughts are important in a classroom discussion, and you hold the key to their self-esteem and further development in the faith. Their confidence depends on your verbal approval.

If you feel you must challenge what they say, do so as you teach, not in direct opposition to what has been volunteered. A younger elementary teacher shared a past experience: "I never spoke during Sunday church school because my second grade teacher once said that my concept of God was immature. I didn't want to be wrong again."

Do prepare many key questions. Prepare open-ended questions that call for expressing feelings, ideas, and creative thoughts. Reword any question that could be answered simply "Yes" or "No." For example, ask, "How would you feel if that happened to you?" or, "Why did the person do that in the story?" or, "How would you have reacted?" These questions could be answered by personal opinions; therefore, the answers would be neither right nor wrong.

Children of all ages can feel important in a discussion if the questions relate to their lives. Interject terms that relate to your particular age group as you prepare the questions so the lesson topic will "scratch them where they itch."

Don't judge the child or youth by his reply. "Jason certainly is weak on his Bible background," Mrs. Thomas, a seventh grade teacher told a friend. "He must have had poor teachers in the past. You should have heard his replies to the questions in class."

It is not the duty of the teacher to judge students. Rather, you are commissioned to teach God's Word and "love them into" a caring relationship with him. If a child does appear weak spiritually, realize that he needs more of your concern and teaching. But do not criticize him to others.

Do listen carefully. Children will feel the Bible and the Christian faith truly have meaning for them when the teacher cares enough to listen. Watch the children as they talk. Be perceptive of any body language they may use to show uncertainty. And listen to their thoughts. Your eye contact and undivided attention will enable the children to gain confidence in themselves. As they feel someone caring enough to listen to them, they will risk speaking out more in class.

Tune in to any clues the children may offer as they contribute to the discussion — a problem at home, insecurity among peers, poor self-esteem. Care enough to let their words open the door to their lives and act accordingly if more action is necessary.

Don't let one child dominate. Serve as the director of the group by encouraging all the children to speak out. Make sure each child has had an opportunity to share his or her feelings and remind the overly zealous child or youth of the need to listen. Help the students to become sensitive to one another by permitting no chatter while a child is talking. Often the teacher may find that "going-around-the-circle" technique is the best way to make certain each child has an opportunity to share.

Do create an atmosphere for God's grace to be shared. When the conversation begins to drag or lull, use this time to share about your own faith in God. Bring in the Scripture passage from the lesson and relate this to the class discussion. Share your own experiences with God and how he moves in your life. If a child expresses a desire for a deeper understanding and commitment, make sure you follow through when the appropriate time comes.

You can best lead a discussion with youth and children by realizing that you are there to help all students "come out of" themselves and share their special uniqueness with the entire class. A discussion with youth and children represents many colors, sizes, and shapes, all sharing and blending. Such a discussion can truly have meaning as young lives are molded and nurtured in the Christian faith.

Youth and adult classes depend on teachers who are caring, prompt, and well-versed in the Bible. But youth and adults also are extremely sensitive to the manner in which the lesson is delivered and the control the teacher exercises over the classroom. In fact, leave it to a perceptive teenager to notice when the teacher is nervous, ill at ease, or unprepared. And how many "borderline" adults simply quit the class when the lesson becomes dull and lifeless?

We have all heard the story of the young child who loudly sang, "Gladly, the Cross-Eyed Bear." Or of the young child who sincerely prayed, "Our Father, who art in Heaven. How did You know my name?"

We usually laugh at these cute anecdotes, thinking they would never occur in our classroom. Yet, the reality is that children, and even adults, do misunderstand words, concepts, and Biblical information vital to their Christian growth.

Perhaps the teacher slurred the words of the song or didn't read the Scripture loudly enough for the class to understand. Maybe a distraction in the classroom kept the pupils from comprehending the correct wording and message.

In the Sunday church school classroom the spoken word conveys the message of Jesus Christ. The teacher attempts to get a response from those in the class — whether by a changed life, dedication of a life to Christ, or even by questions concerning the lesson. If the teacher doesn't speak clearly or enunciate properly, the message goes unheard and lives remain unchanged.

Study the following suggestions for effective speaking in the classroom:

1. *Establish Eye Contact.*

Look at each student as they enter the room and look at the class while you are teaching the curriculum. Eye contact helps to establish a one-to-one relationship with class members. Students will feel trust and warmth as you take time to look into their faces.

2. *Use Body Language.*

Body stance, posture, and facial gestures also assist the spoken word in getting a message across. Body language can enhance your spoken words. You might practice in front of a mirror or with family members as you develop your personal style of teaching and delivery. Do not, of course, become overly conscious about this so that it becomes unnatural.

3. *Look for Stumbling Blocks.*

Watch for peculiar habits or traits which may hinder your delivery. Shaky hands, a quiver in your voice, or a glance at the floor all convey a message of insecurity in your teaching.

It is helpful to know your stumbling blocks and to work on these each week. Set personal goals, such as trying to overcome a selected bad habit for five minutes at a time. As you succeed in conquering it, increase the time you concentrate. Stumbling blocks can become stepping stones as you make yourself aware of them and work continually to control them.

Over fifteen years ago, we began working in the Sunday church school of the local church. Our first Sunday "on the job" was filled with apprehension, yet excitement, toward our new challenge. We both honestly believed that all one had to do to teach Sunday church school was read the material and present the facts to the students — becoming a sort of "liaison officer" between the class and the publisher.

Not long afterwards, we both walked dejectedly out of our respective classrooms, having attempted to teach "our" way. The excitement had somehow turned to despair as we reflected on how much energy had to go into the preparation of a Sunday church school lesson.

Since then, as workers in the local church, we have grown in wisdom and experience that years of "on-the-job training" can give. We see teaching as being part of a team, with God as the educator and the teacher as the co-worker. We have also seen that in the successful classes, the teacher enables the classroom experience to be one filled with joy, caring, and celebration. This responsibility entails more than merely teaching the available curriculum.

Here are some "tips" for teaching children, youth, and adults in a class that is geared for Christian success:

1. *Come with expectation.* The song "Something Good Is Going to Happen to You" fills many hearts with hope and anticipation. You can bring the same expectation and excitement to your classroom as you look for small miracles and affirm them. Remember when Robbie brought you a fresh flower? When Sharon prayed aloud for the first time? When the Curtises began attending class as a couple? Looking hopefully for such little serendipities helps the class to come alive with the love of God.

2. *Be sure to contact students* who were absent the previous Sunday. The teacher's work does not end on Sunday morning. Rather, this job entails ongoing care throughout the week. Phone

calls, cards in the mail, personal letters, and more all add to the relationship between student and teacher.

3. *Arriving early and beginning on time* shows students you care. If you are prompt, you encourage your students to be prompt. If you begin your lesson on time, students will make a point to arrive in time to get in on the craft, story, song, or fellowship. Being late for the class lessens the impact of your teaching.

4. *Plenty of rest on Saturday night* enables you to be more effective in educating class members. Have you ever been taught a lesson by someone who couldn't quite "get it together?" Perhaps he yawned the entire class time. Or maybe she had lost her notes. Plan to retire early Saturday night so you can give your students your best.

5. *Take a day off from teaching* from time to time. Teacher "burnout" happens to the best of us. God's work is important enough for us to feel our best when we are in charge. Allow yourself to take a Sunday morning off to attend class as a student, just to "recharge." Your attitude will be more positive the following week. Of course, you'll want to be certain that your substitute is well-versed in teaching.

6. *Include your pastor* in the Sunday church school program. Sometimes ministers need to feel as though they are wanted. A special invitation carried by a student may help to include him or her. Have a special sharing with the pastor and follow with a celebration in the classroom. When the pastor appears on the layperson's (especially children's) turf, he may begin to seem less unapproachable and more human.

7. *Welcome students* as they arrive and call them by name. Name tags can alleviate the problem if you have a large class. However, when you really begin to know your students, names are just as special as personalities.

8. *Encourage discussion* during study time. Some adults refuse to teach Sunday church school because they feel intimidated, aware as they are that they don't "know all the answers." Encourage discussion and admit it when you don't know an answer (that's a sign of honesty, not weakness). Then seek the answer to the question. You will become more genuine to the students and approachable as you help them find answers.

9. *Avoid open criticism and conflict* in the group. Accentuate the positive and handle discipline problems in a quiet manner. If the disciplined student persists in unacceptable behavior, try to find the root of the problem. Are there family difficulties, health problems, or peer pressures? You represent God to those you teach, thus loving-kindness must be displayed as you educate the students.

10. *Let God use you in the classroom.* Be open to the power of the Holy Spirit as you teach. If you feel a need to pray during the lesson, then pray! If you feel led to sing after the prayer, sing joyously! Avoid becoming so structured with your lesson plan that you ignore such special moments.

11. *Above all, remain approachable* to your students. If your faith seems real to your students, it will be contagious, for they model their lives after you. If you appear too "holy," they will feel too removed from the faith you express.

Practice makes perfect. It's especially true in teaching Sunday church school in Christ's church. Bad habits can be eliminated and good habits can be encouraged as you work diligently on your task as the classroom teacher.

With study, planning, work, prayer, and teaming with God, any Sunday church school teacher can be successful.

Bibliography

1. *Will Our Children Have Faith?*, by John H. Westerhoff, III, The Seabury Press, 1976.
2. *Psychology of Pastoral Care*, Paul E. Johnson, Abingdon Press, Nashville, page 56 (1953).
3. *Forty Ways to Teach in Groups*, Martha M. Leypoldt, Judson Press, Pennsylvania, 1967, page 16.
4. *Growing and Winning Through the Sunday School*, Harry M. Piland, Compiler, Convention Press, 1981, page 178.

Chapter Five

SPIRITUALITY AND SERVICE
Sharing Lives and Caring for Others

The formula for a successful Sunday church school is incomplete without two final ingredients: spirituality and service.

Spirituality involves prayer, worship, meditation, and group devotions. Service is a natural extension of our spirituality, a response of our faith in God. In fact, *mission* is putting the *message* of the *Master* into action.

Let's look at these two aspects of a successful Sunday church school class.

Spirituality

Have you ever noticed the members of your congregation during a morning worship service? While many appear to listen attentively, others are busy daydreaming, looking for a closing hymn, or rattling the printed bulletin as they glance down at their watches. We are not recommending canceling the Sunday morning worship service because of congregation apathy. Rather, we are suggesting that the Sunday church school classroom can enable members to understand and experience worship in a way which enhances the morning service.

In our morning worship, we are in communion with God. We celebrate God in our lives through music, liturgy, prayer, Scripture, and sermon. "Through the experience of worship the unity of human relationships is enhanced in devotion to a creative Spirit of Love who meets us in silence and response to our prayers and hymns in the answering vibrations of larger harmonies. In worship we seek a new perspective to clear the vision of selfish and sordid distortions, to see the eternal purposes of creating values and sharing meanings, to appreciate the infinitely potential worth of every person, and to dedicate ourselves in utter devotion to the cause of unfailing love. From a vivid realization of the redemptive Presence in worship, there may come a new resource for creative living, the divine mood of agape or self-giving love that sets aside calcuating desires for self-advantage and offers the best of what one is and has in an outpouring of affectionate concern and devotion to others."[1]

Worship in the Sunday church school classroom can provide a setting of intimacy and spontaneity that is not usually available in the morning service. It also can give the teacher an opportunity for relating spiritually with the students. Worship in the small group setting can take on new meaning and come alive as members are allowed to plan and lead in the activity.

Perhaps the following suggestions used in the class service can enable your members to experience spirituality in an innovative, worshipful way.

1. *Make the worship personal.* This is the key to involving members as the parts of the class worship speak to specific needs within the room.

Encourage class members to express their own feelings and ideas about worship. Adhere to their suggestions for the style you select. Remember the moment is *theirs* and should speak their language in order to be meaningful to them.

A youth class may choose contemporary songs and poems for the liturgy while an older adult class may feel comfortable with familiar hymns. Worship which is personal will reach out to more class members than will that which is not.

2. Choose an appropriate setting. An unexpected trip to another classroom in the church building, the basement of the facility, or a vacant room lit by candlelight to symbolize the Upper Room may give an aura of wonder and Godliness to class members. Some classes find becoming "one" with nature is conducive to class worship as they use the shore of a lake or a place under the trees in the church garden for their worship times.

The altar for the worship setting can be as simple — yet profound — as a small table with a cross and Bible placed upon it. Candlelight may add sacredness to the special event.

3. Use music that is familiar. Try to keep the worship experience contemporary enough to include the members' favorite songs. Discuss the words before or after they are sung. You might explain theological terms or unfamiliar words that people are confused with. With a children's class, even the simple song "Jesus Loves Me" becomes a topic for explanation as the words sum up the message of the Gospels.

Youth and children's classes may benefit from the use of instruments while they sing. Rhythm instruments can be purchased or made by class members. Guitars, autoharps, and the piano add assurance as they accompany members in singing, yet are not mandatory. In other words, if you do not have access to a musical instrument, try singing acapella!

You may vary the types of songs you use as the tone of your worship service changes. An exuberant hymn used for the gathering, a soft, prayerful song before the message, and a hymn of celebration for the closing all add to the mood of the service. This enables class members to prepare for the different parts of the worship spiritually.

Don't be afraid to interject traditional hymns into your worship. A familiar song from your denomination's heritage will provide a feeling of security as class members draw on their religious roots.

4. Include liturgy and readings. Have different members read the liturgy each time. You can print sheets for the class congregation to respond. Actually liturgy means "the people work." As the teacher, you must try to involve all class members in this time.

Some classes choose to write their own liturgy. Scriptures can be divided into sections with different members participating in a choral reading. Questions that pertain to members' lives with scriptural responses can be read aloud. For example, the following liturgical reading was written by a fourth grade class for use in Sunday church school worship.

Speaker:	*Why am I lonely?*
Group I:	*The Lord will give you comfort.*
Speaker:	*Why am I afraid?*
Group II:	*The Lord will give you strength.*
Speaker:	*Why do I have fears?*
Group III:	*The Lord will give you courage.*
Speaker:	*Then I will turn to him.*
All:	*Go, and he will give you Peace.*

This reading was written after a study on loneliness and fears, offering the hope of our faith. One child was chosen to be the speaker with the rest of the class responding.

Drama can be used effectively in worship times. Role plays, pantomine, puppets, clowns, or interpretive movement help keep the interest of class members. Be sure to allow members time to discuss the meaning of the play, skit, or activity.

5. *Make the message count.* The adult teacher, pastor, or class member can give the message. It can also be a film or a slide show set to music. It is best to keep the message short and to the point keeping in mind the audience at hand.

Try to have a theme for the worship event and use this theme on which to build the message. The theme can be a Scriptural passage such as "God cares for you," or could be on feelings such as loneliness, anxiety, and fears. During the sermon, the leader should touch base with life issues that the members are confronted with — death, separation, rejection — and offer the hope of the Christian faith. Remember to "scratch them where they itch" when choosing sermon ideas, offering insight and guidance that meets their personal needs.

6. *Allow time for sharing*. Worship in the classroom should be a time to celebrate being together. But in this celebration it is also necessary to listen to one another and bear one another's burdens in a *koinonia* of concern and trust.

Allow for freedom and flexibility in this part of the service. Realizing that expressing feelings is difficult for many people, you will need to put class members at ease. You may have to begin the sharing by expressing your feelings about the group, your life, and your own personal faith.

Some groups always close with a group sharing time. A lot of hard feelings are forgotten during this moment, friendships renewed, and love and affirmation shared.

7. *Prayer is vital*. Always begin and end with a prayer time in the class worship. Encouraging the class members to pray is not a difficult task if prayer is introduced as a "conversation" with God.

Prayers may be written during the class period and read aloud at the end of worship. This works well with older children and youth as they become more intimidated by their peers.

A type of responsive prayer can be used even with the youngest group of children. The teacher may ask the group to repeat a phrase together such as "We Thank Thee, Lord," after each section of the prayer.

Other innovative ideas for worship in the Sunday church school classroom include using arts and crafts, banners, and other tools to express feelings. Children, youth, and adults can participate in painting to sacred music, making colorful banners to show a theme or liturgical season, and molding clay as they listen to a story.

In the Sunday church school classroom, worship can take place at any time. Yet, because worship consists of sharing God's love, it usually is an experience we build up to at the end of classtime, providing a fitting conclusion to our morning of study, recreation, and group building.

As the most significant event for the body of believers in the Christian church, worship is a vital experience. Yet, it need not be laborious or boring for class members. As we pause during class time to sing, pray, and praise God, we can offer ongoing Christian nurture to those we teach You can enable your class members to understand and get more from corporate worship by designing services that speak to them, that are a part of them.

Prayer in the Classroom

Spirituality includes encouraging Bible study, prayer, and devotions for class members, not only in Sunday church school, but also during the week. A strong devotional and prayer life is important for students. A devotional life provides a sense of the transcendent and "other" which helps individuals feel good about themselves, about life, and about God.

Teachers can encourage students to an active prayer life by living what they teach and sharing their experiences with the students. Praying frequently in class, encouraging students to have a special prayer time and asking for personal requests all help to develop this discipline.

An elementary teacher disclosed to a friend; "Sure I pray in the Sunday church school classroom. But I'm not sure if anyone else is in prayer with me."

We can find tremendous power in prayer. And what better place to express this power than at Christ's church. Maxie Dunnam describes the human need for prayer in *Workbook of Living Prayer.* He says, "As living beings, we breathe, we eat, we drink, we sleep. As human beings, we breathe, eat, drink, sleep, and pray. It's part of our nature as human beings to pray."[2]

There are some helpful techniques you can use in the classroom to enable prayer to become an integral part of your Sunday church school lesson. Perhaps these suggestions can assist you.

1. *Pray at a regular time each week.* Establishing a routine is vital in order for class members to participate in the prayer experience. Most teachers find prayer helpful to begin the class period, asking for God's guidance. This opening prayer should be used to gather students into a more worshipful frame of mind as they end their fellowship time and begin to learn from the lesson. It is often easy to say, "We've got to move on and begin the lesson" and

cancel the opening prayer. But this communication with God can often set the spiritual tone for the class session.

2. *Encourage sharing during the prayer time.* A Sunday church school class can be a support group for children, youth, and adults. As we gather for study and fellowship with other Christians, we should also feel free to express concerns, needs, and problems in our lives. Personal joys can include answers to prayers, goals met, or relationships that have been enhanced. Concerns include praying for those who are ill, personal stumbling blocks, or class conflict. This prayer time is often best placed during a class worship, toward the end of class time.

3. *Teach class members to pray.* Often youth and children have a difficult time expressing their feelings openly with God and others. You can enable them to learn how to pray by writing open-ended sentences on the board and letting the children or youth fill in the blanks verbally.

For example:
I am happy about ______________________________.
I am thankful for ______________________________.
I am sad about ______________________________.
I worry about ______________________________.
I want to pray for ______________ because ______________.

As you lead the members in filling in the blanks, they are establishing communication with God that will enhance their personal prayer life.

4. *Expect miracles to happen.* Prayer is communication with a living God. And answers should be expected. Bring an atmosphere of anticipation to your Sunday church school class as you pray together. Share answers to prayer you have experienced and encourage class members to do the same. A prayer list on the blackboard will help members see how God meets requests prayed for. Check the names and concerns from time to time and talk about the miracle of prayer.

5. *Talk in a language class members can understand.* The Bible instructs us to "Come like a child to the Father." Our prayers with children need to be simple and spoken with words they can understand. Try to avoid symbolic terminology such as "magnify" or "light," words young children probably do not understand. Class members of all ages need to learn that God is loving like a father, caring like a mother, and understanding like a faithful best friend. This helps students to respect God's awesome power, yet trust him enough to want to share everyday concerns.

6. *Be creative in prayer.* A simple song can be a powerful prayer if the attitude is right. A litany describing feelings on a specific topic can be read by all class members. A Scripture can be read as a prayer that pertains to the lesson. By not limiting the types of prayer, we can expand the ways we talk with God.

7. *Spend time listening to God.* Often we become so involved with pouring out our troubles and woes that we forget to listen for answers. Remember, God speaks to us in many ways. The Bible tells of God speaking in dreams, visions, and images. Jesus told of God dwelling "within." You need, therefore, to train your students to take time to be still, to hear God speaking. This could be through Scriptures, intuition, or in still other ways.

8. *Live a life of prayer.* It is extremely difficult to be in a prayerful frame of mind on Sunday morning if prayer is not included in the other six days. Living a life filled with God's love and in communion with him is vital. As a Sunday church school teacher, you have the commission to live such a life lest your teachings become hypocritical.

The Bible is the most powerful prayer book we have. In this holy book we find Scriptures encouraging us to pray, teaching us how to pray, providing examples of prayer, and giving us answers to our prayers. In Mark 11:24 we read, "Therefore, I tell you, whatever you ask in prayer, believe that you receive it, and you will." In John 16:24 we read, "Hitherto you have asked nothing in my name; ask and you will receive, that your joy may be full." (RSV)

God calls us to pray, for without prayer our life lacks divine direction. When we pray, we acknowledge that God is a vital part of our life. And teaching class members how to pray through example in the Sunday church school classroom is one of the most beneficial lessons we can share.

Service

Service and Christian mission are at the very heart of our Christian faith. Jesus said that we will be held accountable before God for how we treat "the least of these." A faith that is not directed outward is no faith at all. As Christians, we need to realize that love must flow through us into acts and deeds of kindness.

Jesus calls us to make disciples of all nations, to minister to the hungry, to the naked, to those in prison, to others in need. As we create an awareness of mission and service in our classrooms, we need to broaden our horizons to include:

- An awareness of all people on earth — the rich, the poor, those of different backgrounds and creeds, all nationalities, male, female, those we know and those we don't know.
- A realization of God's love for all humankind — not merely for church people and those who are professed Christians.
- An involvement with, and ongoing projects for, persons in need in our church, community, nation, and world.

A Sunday church school class should begin its involvement in Christian mission right at home. It is helpful to let the class members see, do, and be personally involved in some type of project where they can see results. As the class members mature and realize greater needs around and beyond them, you can move to adopt projects to assist people across the seas.

Service to others puts the Gospel message into action. Service projects can be initiated by any age group, from preschool up. Assuring that the project is suited for the group and that growth will occur, however, requires careful planning and implementation.

Perhaps the following ideas can guide your class's plans for a service project.

1. Discover your group's needs. Brainstorm with the members of your class, and write down all responses. Discuss what talents you have within the class's membership. What are the strengths? Weaknesses? Will the entire department make a commitment to participate along with the class or will the group be small? Do class members want to choose a long-term or short-term project?

Once the class has identified talents and limitations, discuss needs in the local church, the community, and the world. Do the class's talents fit into any one area? An elementary class may choose to sing at a retirement home once a month. Because of the limitations of age and maturity, this project would be best as a short-term service attempt.

An adult department may decide to paint the church, raise money for a foreign missions project or visit shut-ins. They could tackle something long-term.

2. Take appropriate action. After selecting the project and determining that it is compatible with your class members' skills, set group goals for the particular project by answering the following questions: (1) What is to be accomplished? (2) Who will be in charge? (3) Who will participate? (4) When will the project take place? (5) What is the completion date? (6) What factors may hinder the project? (7) What factors will benefit the project?

Involve as many people as possible in the class project. Other church members may have skills which could be used in implementing the task. For instance, some people can offer financial assistance or help with child care during the event. Others will offer spiritual strength through study and prayer.

3. Reflect on what is taking place. Periodically sit back and look at the action taking place. Are lives being changed? Are your members able to witness more freely to those around them? Reflection helps the group to understand that ministry means doing for others.

4. Evaluate the project results. Did the project work out as anticipated? Did every member pull his weight? What could have made the planning or implementation smoother?

Evaluation is vital to understanding the procedures necessary for ministry. However, your members should remember to keep their evaluations positive and task-oriented rather than negatively critical.

Keep a folder or notebook listing the steps the group took. Refer to this list as other projects are undertaken.

Here are some other ideas for enabling class members to become enthusiastic about service:

Provide props for group use. A folder with appropriate slots to place a "dime a day" can be a way members save money for a specific project. A bank decorated to look like a village hut may symbolize the need for funds to support a refugee project. One congregation had a large picture of a cow with a metal bucket on a table nearby in hopes of collecting enough money to buy a heifer to supply milk for needy children in a remote area.

You may also create awareness for mission through teaching aids. Ideas such as maps in the classroom "mission corner," globes with flags pinned on locations where the church is in mission, or a bulletin board where letters from area missionaries are posted can be useful. Show films and slides to let class members see the living conditions of the mission field. And go on field trips to local places where mission support is needed.

Service projects can give classes an opportunity to join together to help others. Adopting a family in the community, raising funds for a medical van in Haiti, or planting trees in the wastelands of a far-off country are all mission work in action. Adults can give leadership and guidance to service projects while youth and children add their enthusiasm. And all receive understanding and training as they assist in projects as a team.

It has been said that service is "putting feet to our faith." Service to all God's people is our response to what we have learned and experienced in our Sunday church school classrooms. By "doing" for others, we are truly involved in ministry instead of merely talking about it.

Has your class reached the point of putting their faith into action? You can help stimulate this mission-mindedness as you enable class members to become aware of all God's children.

Bibliography

1. *Psychology of Pastoral Care*, Paul E. Johnson, Abingdon, Nashville, Tennessee, 1953, page 132.
2. *The Workbook of Living Prayer*, Maxie Dunnam, The Upper Room, Nashville, Tennessee, 1974, page 12.

Chapter Six

GOAL SETTING
The Key to a Successful Teacher

Sunday morning is a busy time in our home. Preparing sermons, shuffling Sunday church school books, dressing children, and meeting a tight schedule in order to arrive in time for class is difficult each week.

Yet, in the midst of this Sunday morning confusion, we always allow for some personal time to pray for guidance and to review teaching goals.

Goals are vital for Sunday church school teachers: They help turn hopes and dreams into purpose. Without specific goals, the teacher has no guideline by which to measure growth — quantitative or qualitative.

Goals are especially helpful for the classroom teacher when attendance becomes stagnant or when enthusiasm declines. Teachers can evaluate their goals periodically and determine what changes need to be made.

The following steps could assist you in starting the teaching year with goals that speak to your class.

1. *Ask yourself: What would I like to see happen in my class?*

Dream. Brainstorm. Picture your class a year from now. What

do you visualize? Perhaps an increase in size, winning more persons to the Christian faith, or seeing spiritual maturity in your present students. Maybe your dream is more specific, such as helping Sarah overcome her shyness or helping Bart to get along better with other students.

Write down these dreams, for they can become reality in the near future.

2. *Ask yourself: What would it take to make these visions into realities?*

Now, list on paper the planning steps that could help meet these problems head-on. Perhaps ongoing visitation, telephoning, or sending notes in the mail could help to increase the size of your group. Showing care toward each member would encourage regular attendance.

More Bible study during the class time — relating the Scripture to life situations — might help the students see the Christian life as a winning lifestyle. Teaching lessons on witnessing — how to explain the faith, how to lead others into a loving relationship with God — could open new doors for the students. This not only can help their own understanding, but could help when they try to share their faith with someone else.

Specific personal goals can be met by seeking help for students with problems. Affirming a student is one way of helping him overcome insecurity. Local Christian professionals can assist you in aiding learners with learning disabilities, family problems, depression, and other difficulties.

3. *Review your goals weekly.*

Goals you set give purpose to your teaching. Suppose your class dwindles from ten students to four. What has gone wrong? Perhaps more teacher visitation is needed. Or suppose Sarah, the shy child, grows more timid than ever? Perhaps increased one-to-one interaction, with special encouragement, is needed.

Reviewing your goals regularly helps you to see which have been reached. Your faith will be strengthened as lives change before your eyes.

4. *Evaluate the goals as class needs change.*

"I've worked so hard at getting Robert to open up in the classroom," one teacher shared. "Now I've got to help him learn there are times to listen!"

Sometimes goals must be adjusted. Perhaps your emphasis for a successful Sunday church school class has been on numerical growth. Now the class is large but needs nurture, intensive Bible study, and personal care. New goals must be set.

Perhaps a new student has come into your class from a troubled background. Could she have a place on your goal sheet?

Goals set with God's love in mind need not be extravagant. Rather, these aims are set to produce balanced growth in your students — emotional, spiritual, academic, and social.

Here are some goals which we decided to set for ourselves for the upcoming Sunday church school year. Might they help *you* create your own guidelines for teaching? Read them thoughtfully; then think about your own classroom situation. How similar are these goals to your own?

I pledge to:

1. Present the Word of God in a way students can understand through drama, creative art, role play, and other methods.
2. Be a caring Christian example, showing concern by mailing absentee cards, making home visits, having a Coke or meal with each student.
3. Teach caring, sensitivity, and cooperation with others by presenting conflict situations, using role play, and reinforcing the Biblical challenge Christ teaches.
4. Let God speak through me during class time after listening to God through prayer and seeking beauty in each student.
5. Allow time each week for personal decisions for Christ — through quiet moments, sharing of joys and concerns, planned worship in the classroom.

6. Help each student see the Christian faith as a celebration, and having a full life, by enjoying the fun in classtime and having several socials for the class members.
7. Help one student become involved with other class members, involving this person in group activities and encouraging others to befriend the student.
8. Help one student going through a family crisis by giving extra comfort and assurance, listening and seeking help if necessary.

The success of your Sunday church school class depends on how seriously you address the personal needs of your class members, and on regular, constant prayer and communication with God.

Remember, success is defined as "a favorable result, a good fortune." And Sunday church school classes which are experiencing these successful results are motivated and nurtured by teachers who really care.

How will you go to class this Sunday? Prepared to teach? Or prepared to change lives?

The decision is up to you!

Questions Christian Educators Ask

Here are some frequently asked questions concerning the planning and development of an effective Sunday church school program. Study the answers as you plan your teaching.

Q. I know Sunday church school is beneficial to children as they learn about the Gospel, but why is it so important for adults? Can't we merely study the Bible at home?

A. Some adults feel that a commitment to the Lord and to studying the Bible is sufficient for growing in the Christian faith. We have experienced that a commitment to a Sunday church school class, a specific body of believers, is also important to complete and complement this bond. There are several reasons for this.

Class membership means being accountable by serving on committees, finding our talents and using them in the class and attending faithfully.

This commitment to a class will enhance your relationship with other Christians and with Christ. As you learn to listen to the ideas of others and compromise in making decisions, you will learn acceptance.

Studying the Scriptures with others gives insight into life.

Through God's Word, you are able to understand each person in the class and find suggestions for living a more Christlike life. The beauty of searching God's Word within the fellowship of a Sunday church school class is that people are able to share how he has revealed himself in their lives. We can learn from the experience of other Christians around us.

A Sunday church school class is a supportive community. Believers support each other in the face of death, trials, and family crises. Joy is celebrated by all members in this community. And the growing friendships are not hindered by age or sex barriers. Caring relationships are experienced in the Sunday church school by singles and couples of all ages.

Through a Sunday church school class, members are challenged to change their life-style. Confrontations with Christ and the gospel can result and faith be deepened as they meet for fellowship and study.

Some adults who merely attend the weekly worship service claim that Sunday church school is "just for kids." But our need for constant nurture and encouragement in the faith continues. A Sunday church school class can provide just that!

Q. When do you know it is time to start a new class? How can you do this?

A. It is time to start a new class when you have difficulty getting newcomers into your adult class. Perhaps you're finding a lack of interest due to extremes in ages or curriculum differences. In any case, when all efforts fail to boost Sunday church school attendance and class participation begins to level off, most likely it is time to start a new class.

The following steps outline an effective procedure in planning a new class.

1. Recruit a core group.

This group of leaders should include members from a present class, along with other adults who have expressed interest in the new class. This small group will serve as the backbone of the new class. By combining the present leaders with new leaders on the committee, you will be able to have both experience and new ideas with which to work.

The first step is to establish the need for the upcoming class. Questions must be answered such as: Who needs the class? Which age-group will be attracted? What are the concerns and the issues of that particular age-group? Once you are able to speak specifically to a particular group's needs, the core group can most effectively recommend teachers and curriculum.

Have the core group select a study course with which to begin the class. This group may also set goals, such as attendance and membership figures, as well as benefits they would hope the new class would offer.

The last planning step should be to select a kickoff time and date. Make sure this does not conflict with any event on the church calendar. Then launch out in faith.

2. Publicize.

Publicity should include brochures, mailings, phone calls, and personal home visits to interested persons who do not attend a Sunday church school class. The pastor is vital in publicizing the new class. He or she can provide many contacts and can suggest innovative program ideas. The pastor should ideally teach the class periodically.

3. The first day of class.

On the first morning of the new class be sure to allow ample fellowship time. Coffee and doughnuts may encourage late sleepers.

Allow the teacher ample time to guide the scripture study and encourage participation. Avoid challenging the opinions of the new members until a true fellowship is established.

4. Ask for Feedback.

Response is vital in the early stages of a new class. Did the lessons meet the needs of the age-group? Were the members made comfortable by the teacher and hosting committee?

Follow through with phone calls and letters to newcomers for a few weeks until a Sunday church school habit is formed. Then, use the proven formula for success — C.A.R.E.S. — to continue the nurture and development of the class.

Q. What can Sunday church school leaders do when the enthusiasm of the teachers and workers declines?

A. Teaching is not easy and should never be taken lightly. In 1 Corinthians 12:28 and Ephesians 4:11 Paul affirms the teacher as a vital part of the church. And for those who do commit themselves to being a teacher, the rewards are tremendous. But often in a Sunday church school program communication problems can occur which can stifle teachers and lessen enthusiasm.

A survey may help relieve this problem. The following questions comprised an attitude and opinion survey that several area churches used. You might find it beneficial for use in your own situation.

1. Why did you agree to teach in the Sunday church school program?
2. Do you completely understand your job description?
3. Do you understand the needs and characteristics of the age-group you are teaching?
4. Do you have difficulty using the curriculum? If so, do you need more resources?
5. Do you need an assistant or helper to complete your teaching team?
6. Would a caring/sharing group of teachers which meets on a regular basis before Sunday church school be beneficial to you?
7. List any problems — behavioral, planning, speaking — for which you need solutions.
8. Do you need more classroom input from the pastor?

After submitting the teacher survey and receiving the answers, evaluate the needs of your teachers. A workshop may be helpful in offering more "how to" information to increase teacher know-how and enthusiasm.

Here are some sample workshop topics:

1. *Lesson Planning and Preparation* — how to plan; praying for guidance; Bible study; gathering supplies and materials.
2. *Follow-Up* — visitation; cards in the mail; phoning; pastoral input; seeking professional advice.
3. *Time Involved In Teaching* — planning; coming early to greet students; setting up the classroom; responsibilities outside the class.
4. *Student/Teacher Relationships* — class fellowship times; seasonal parties; spiritual life retreats.
5. *Available Resources* — films; filmstrips; tapes; church leaders; outside speakers.
6. *Teacher Requirements* — teacher planning meetings; worker training courses; workshops.
7. *Classroom Responsibilities* — bulletin boards; visual and audio displays; cleanup.

A workshop may help teachers to better comprehend the extent of their role. Be sure to allow time to question the commitment. You will find that apathy will turn to enthusiasm as communication improves.

Q. *How can you involve more parents and adults in the Sunday church school program on a short-term or long-term basis?*

A. A parent-involvement group may enable you to depend on more adults in your program. This group of adults can meet periodically to share problems, receive support, and find answers. But their main purpose should be to serve as assistants in the church school program — morning, evening, and weekly. In fact, if the job of the church is to train and build disciples, then we must join forces with the family, especially the parents, and become partners in developing youth and children, helping them to form their own attitudes and decisions, and molding them into responsible Christian adults.

Parents and volunteer adults can offer many assets to a Sunday church school program. Churches use these adults in the following ways:

1. *Program resource persons* — being available as resource persons when their talents or vocational skills are needed; assisting in picking up films or other literature for teachers to use; contacting professionals to come and speak to various groups in the Sunday church school.

2. *Transportation* — providing rides to group activities, projects, parties, retreats; bring children, youth, and adults to Sunday church school or other church functions.

3. *Gifts* — giving funds and supplies; sponsoring scholarships for children, youth, young adults to go to various workshops, retreats, camps.

4. *Chaperone* — offering assistance to classroom teachers by "being there," being an "extra body" at retreats, socials, projects.

5. *"Offering home"* — making the home available for socials, parties, Bible studies, counseling.

6. *Calling* — reminding children, youth, adults, of up-coming events, making arrangements for trips and socials, following through on absentees for large classes.

7. *Assisting in worship* — sharing one's own faith by verbal witness; providing Communion elements, such as baking homemade bread for the common loaf.

8. *Helping with service projects* — assisting in the planning and

implementation of service projects with community agencies and other groups.

9. *Representing the class* — supporting the class by representing them on church committees which can help them acquire broader programming (such as hiring a youth director, obtaining handbells for the children's choir, seeking another classroom in the church building.)

In recruiting parents to become active members of the parent involvement or support group, you must remind them of the overall benefits. A deeper relationship between the parent and child can be established, which can, in itself, teach the power of Christ's love. It is easier to secure volunteers to serve on a weekly basis or other short-term basis rather than for an entire year or quarter. Such participation enables parents to see what is going on in their young people's lives by watching them interact with peers and hearing the discussions in which they participate. Parent support also enables the parent to fulfill the need to serve and use his or her talents in the local church. Through the parent support group, relationship problems can be dealt with using ideas from other parents, and the parents can truly feel that they are important as a vital resource in developing their child's identity.*

Q. *What about classroom safety for younger children?*

A. Here are some suggestions for increasing safety in nursery and pre-school rooms:

1. Check your room for safety periodically. It is vital that the classroom teacher evalute the room from the child's eye level. Check the floor for tattered carpet or loose tile. Are there splinters in wooden tables and chairs? Exposed nails are another hazard found in many classrooms.

**Youth Leader*, "Organizing a Parent Support Group" by Debra Fulghum Bruce, Frances Brooke, editor. Board of Discipleship, Nashville. Winter 81-82, pp. 8 and 9.

Thumbtacks are a common source of accidents. Frequently these sharp pins fall on the floor and are found later in a child's foot. Do you have a sink in your room? Make sure that the water temperature is set low enough to prevent scalding. And be sure all electrical outlets and appliances are working properly. A short in a lamp plug can be disastrous.

2. Don't leave potentially dangerous items within a child's reach. Objects which could become weapons — scissors, paint brushes, pencils — should be locked away. Prevention is the key to protecting children from undue harm.

3. Talk openly with your class about safety rules. An elementary age-group could write their own list of rules, such as: "Don't run in the hallway or classroom. Don't leave craft tools on the table or floor. Keep all four chair legs on the floor." If the rules are clearly stated, there is less chance for an accident.

If children defiantly break a rule, discuss this with them immediately. They endanger not only themselves but also the safety of their classmates.

4. Don't panic should a mishap occur. Remain calm and concerned. Avoid hysteria. Is there a doctor or nurse in a nearby class who would be available to assist in an emergency? Keep an emergency phone number handy. Preparedness is essential in acting quickly when a mishap occurs.

5. Be acquainted with emergency procedures. Every church should have several clearly labeled first-aid kits in the building. All adult leaders and teachers should be aware of their locations. Encourage some teachers to take the Red Cross first-aid or CPR courses. The usefulness of such classes may seem limited, but one serious accident more than makes the effort worthwhile.

Have a good how-to-first-aid book available. *A Sigh of Relief — The First-Aid Handbook For Childhood Emergencies*, by Kenneth Jay Solomon, M.D., is an excellent resource. Also, have the phone numbers of the local police, fire department, ambulance, and Poison

Control Center written by each telephone. Always ask a professional before using any poison antidotes.

6. Don't leave students unattended. Most home accidents occur when the parent runs to answer the phone or door for "just a second." In the classroom while you are caring for many young lives, it is vital to have a teacher's helper around — just in case!

Q. If you could sum it up, what is the teacher's main function?

A. In John 10:3 we read, "The gatekeeper opens the gate for him; the sheep hear his voice as he calls his own sheep by name, and he leads them out." We can picture the gatekeeper keeping track of all the sheep, large and small, young and old, as they enter the pasture for grazing. Most shepherds verify that if one sheep becomes lost or hurt along the way, they will leave the herd to go comfort it.

In the Sunday church school classroom, the teacher serves as the gatekeeper as he or she oversees the classroom activities. Not only does the gatekeeper make sure that the lesson is presented or that a verse is understood, this person also checks constantly to see who is being included, who is being left out and who is hurting.

One boy in our congregation told his mother that his Sunday church school class smiled. "And, my teacher really knows my name," Tracy said as he beamed about his "special" class.

In order to be a gatekeeper you must develop a caring, warm environment in the classroom, creating a room that "smiles." The teacher who chooses to fulfill this Biblical role assures that the environment in the room on Sunday morning is conducive to the sharing of God's grace. Faith in Jesus Christ, our ultimate goal for our students, will be the result.

Ask yourself: Is my classroom inviting? A gatekeeper should be certain that the total layout of the class is warm and welcoming. A Sunday church school classroom which is dull, lacking an appealing bulletin board and chair arrangement, will destroy the environment you seek to create.

Go through the room before the students arrive and check its appearance. Arrange the chairs in comfortable seating order. Tidy up the table tops. Arrange shelves attractively.

First impressions *do* make a difference to students. When they enter a room where someone, a gatekeeper, has taken the time to straighten up, set out the lesson, and display pictures at their eye level, they feel welcome. They interpret the clean room as Tracy did — as a room that "smiled."

As a gatekeeper, do you arrive before your students? A teacher speaks of a time when she was in second grade. "I arrived early that morning because my mother had to prepare for communion. I remember sitting in the dark classroom feeling very alone and afraid. When she did come in, the teacher was in such a hurry trying to make up for lost time, she barely noticed me. As she rushed about putting up pictures and writing on the board, I remember my temporary feelings of distrust and anger toward her and toward the church."

A good shepherd always wakes before his sheep to make sure they follow him on the day's journey. In John 10:4a we read, "And when he putteth forth his own sheep, he goeth before them."

It takes self-discipline for a Sunday church school teacher to become a gatekeeper. Wakening early on Sunday morning, having prayer and study with God, then arriving before the students, takes a special commitment. But, the benefits are great: you are able to provide security and peace to the students as they arrive.

Plan special activities, crafts, or creative involvement for early birds. Every moment is vital as you serve as a messenger for Christ.

Be sure you really know your students. A shepherd develops a special relationship with his sheep because of the amount of time they spend together. Twelve hours together daily on the pasture fields enhance their relationship. By contrast, only one hour in the Sunday church school classroom hardly gives the teacher ample time to truly understand the students.

In John 10:3b we read, "And, the sheep hear his voice . . . and he calleth his own sheep by name."

Can you call your students by name? If you were to lead them, would they feel close enough to you to follow? Be consistent in planning times each week when you get to know your students. Follow-up weekly on absentees and visitors.

A friend shared that her son was in the local paper for winning a spelling contest at school. "Would you believe that his pre-school Sunday church school teacher sent a congratulatory card to him?" she asked in amazement. "She was Don's teacher four years ago and never stops caring!"

Being the gatekeeper means overseeing all in the classroom. Has a clique developed among members? Is someone being excluded? It is your responsibility to step in and help everyone be included in God's house. Someone has described the gatekeeper as a person with "eyes in the back of his head." Actually, in order to be a fair, concerned teacher, you must draw on all of your special resources, using foresight and hindsight.

A special environment where God's love can be felt can only be created if the teacher is perceptive enough to make everyone feel included.

Your rewards, as the gatekeeper, come when you do all you can to let God's love shine through you. Knowing this, you can put the class in God's hands. This is the key to successful teaching!